"Read this book if you want to throw lig
merely more heat. Dr. Hoffmeier's biblical
national borders, guest workers, the differ
eigners in Old Testament times, and many

—MARVIN OLASKY, Editor-in-Cl
Provost, The King's College, New York City

"Doubtless some will question this or that detail of his reading of Scripture, but Hoffmeier's book is a very healthy antidote to the merely sentimental readings that dominate much Christian thought on this complex and challenging issue."

—D. A. CARSON, Research Professor of New Testament,
Trinity Evangelical Divinity School

"*The Immigration Crisis* offers biblical perspectives on how Christians might respond to the complex needs and challenges that legal and illegal immigration pose. Dr. James Hoffmeier's knowledge of the ancient Near East unlocks the door to the biblical wisdom that shaped Israel's compassionate response to this timeless issue. You will discover how love and compassion for immigrants involves so much more than building or removing walls and deciding who receives or is denied amnesty."

—REV. VIN UPHAM, Pastor, Immanuel Baptist Church,
New Hartford, NY

"Hoffmeier has produced an authoritative work on what the Bible does and does not say about immigration. He allows the Bible to speak for itself within its cultural context without reading modern politics into the text. While his knowledge of the biblical text and the greater ancient Near East set the groundwork for an accurate hermeneutical approach, his sensitivity to the issues provides a road map for the church to stay true to its biblical roots while serving its calling to be a light to the nations."

—STEVEN M. ORTIZ, Associate Professor of Archaeology and Biblical
Backgrounds, Southwestern Baptist Theological Seminary

"Dr. Hoffmeier has written with insight and balance. There is biblical compassion and legal accountability throughout the pages of this engaging journey of history and culture. This book should provoke meaningful discussion among civil and church leaders on this timely topic of immigration."

—ROGER HABER, Senior Pastor, Central Baptist Church,
Middleboroughm Massachusetts

"I come from a troubled nation from which hundreds of thousands of people have emigrated to western nations some legally and some illegally. Many have done so because of genuine pain, danger, or need they have experienced in Sri Lanka. I have always discouraged people from using illegal means to do this and often preached about this in Sri Lanka. I resonate fully with the dual biblical emphasis presented in this book of caring for the alien and of submitting to the laws of the land."

—AJITH FERNANDO, National Director, Youth for Christ,
Sri Lanka

"With his book *The Immigration Crisis: Immigrants, Aliens, and the Bible,* Jim Hoffmeier has done the church a real service. He brings the Word of God to bear on one of the most pressing political and social issues of our day. Hoffmeier himself is especially well-equipped to bring us guidance on this issue. His own life, family, and career have been deeply intertwined with the issues of immigrants and aliens. Coupled with his long and fruitful career as a Biblical scholar, Hoffmeier has the tools to help us. A real strength of the book is its panoramic view of the entire canon. Certainly those of us who follow Christ need biblical light to shine on these pressing questions of our day. I would highly recommend Jim Hoffmeier's work as a wonderful starting place for developing a biblical perspective on the immigration crisis."

—VIC GORDON, Senior Pastor, Beachpoint Church,
Fountain Valley, California

"Conscientious Christians seeking to formulate a Christian response to illegal immigration will be much aided by Dr. Hoffmeier's work. He presents a careful consideration of the Hebrew language and context that aid the reader in understanding the Old Testament distinction between an alien and a foreigner. He then helpfully offers possible ways to apply these concepts to the current discussion. This former immigrant is grateful for the clarity and insight he brings to this important issue."

—LAURA C. MIGUÉLEZ, Assistant Professor of Theology,
Wheaton College

"How can we resolve the immigration crisis in America today with humane sensitivity but with respect for the rule of law? James Hoffmeier brings the clarity and structure of biblical society to the confusion and chaos of modern America. He is one of the rare scholars and thinkers who listens to the Bible and does not tell the Bible what it should say. He hears the Bible speaking about the true meaning of sanctuary and of being a part of a society rather than a stranger. As a rabbi, I have shared Hoffmeier's conclusions with members of my Jewish community who are fascinated and open to hear the message of this provocative and intellectually stimulating book. For anyone who believes in the Judeo-Christian way of life, this book is essential reading. I wish that we could have more books like this on the other important controversies of our time."

—RABBI BENJAMIN SCOLNIC, Temple Beth Sholom, Hamden,
Connecticut; Adjunct Professor, Southern Connecticut State University

"By exploring the Hebrew Bible's view on immigrants' privileges, Hoffmeier effectively guides the reader through both a descriptive (what/how did God command Israel to treat its immigrants?) and a prescriptive (how people, in today's context, ought to treat its immigrants) process. I strongly recommend this helpful book to those seeking a biblical response."

—DANIEL L. KIM, Assistant Professor of Old Testament,
Covenant Seminary, St. Louis

# THE IMMIGRATION CRISIS

# THE IMMIGRATION CRISIS

## Immigrants, Aliens, and the Bible

JAMES K. HOFFMEIER

CROSSWAY
WHEATON, ILLINOIS

*The Immigration Crisis*



Published by Crossway
1300 Crescent Street
Wheaton, Illinois 60187



Cover design: J. McGrath

Cover photos: Veer & iStock

First printing, 2009

Printed in the United States of America

All emphases in Scripture quotations have been added by the author.



ISBN PDF: 978-1-4335-0608-6

ISBN Mobipocket: 978-1-4335-0609-3

**Library of Congress Cataloging-in-Publication Data**

Hoffmeier, James Karl, 1951–
The immigration crisis : immigrants, aliens & the Bible / James K. Hoffmeier
p. cm.
Includes bibliographical references and index.
ISBN 978-1-4335-0607-9 (tpb)
1. Emigration and immigration in the Bible. 2. Emigration and immigration—Religious aspects—Christianity. II. Title
BS680.E38H64 2009
220.8'305906912—dc22 2008044151

CH 21 20 19 18 17 16 15 14 13 12
15 14 13 12 11 10 9 8 7 6 5 4 3 2

In loving memory of my
mother-in-law and father-in-law

Miriam Fong Tom
(1929–2000)
and
Alfred Lung Yu Tom
(1920–2006)

# CONTENTS

# LIST OF ILLUSTRATIONS

# ABBREVIATIONS

**ESV** English Standard Version (2001)

**JB** Jerusalem Bible (1966)

**KB** Ludwig Koehler and Walter Baumgartner, *Lexicon in Veteris Testamenti Libros* (translated and updated by M.E.J. Richardson [Leiden: Brill, 2001])

**KJV** King James Version (1611)

**NASB** New American Standard Bible (1971)

**NEB** New English Bible (1961)

**NIDOTTE** Willem VanGemeren, ed., *New International Dictionary of Old Testament Theology and Exegesis*, 5 vols. (Grand Rapids, MI: Zondervan, 1997)

**NIV** New International Version (1978)

**NJB** New Jerusalem Bible (1985)

**NJPS** New Jewish Publication Society Version (1985)

**NRSV** New Revised Standard Version (1989)

**RSV** Revised Standard Version (1952)

**TLV** Today's Living Version (1996)

**TNIV** Today's New International Version (2005)

# PREFACE

George was shivering. I thought perhaps it was because it was a cold, snowy night in Toronto; after all, he was from the Caribbean. But when he started to tell me his story, I understood his trepidation. At the time I was a landed immigrant, which meant I had the equivalent of a green card in Canada. He had sought me out at a church we both attended; I was on the leadership team for the college and career group. George was trembling because he had overstayed his visitor's visa and feared deportation. He desperately wanted to stay and seek the better life that Canada afforded him. The law required George to apply for immigrant status outside of the country, but he felt that if he left he might not get it. He also knew that if he were deported, he would never get back in. So he came to me for counsel. "What should I do?" he asked.

I felt for George. His dilemma was real. My instincts told me he should do what was right and legal and trust that things would work out for him. So I helped him think through his options and encouraged him to leave Canada and apply for landed status. I never saw George again. I was not sure if he had gone underground or left the country. More than a decade later I met a mutual friend and asked him, "What happened to George?" He told me that George did indeed get his resident status and was living in western Canada. It was good to hear that he did the right thing, followed the law, and things had worked out for him.

Since my encounter with George I have had occasion to advise others about their legal status in the U.S.A. One reason I understand some of the issues for aliens is that I have spent many years of my life living as an immigrant. As I already mentioned, I was a legal immigrant in Canada, a standing I had for more than a decade. Prior to that, I had spent most of my first sixteen years in Egypt. My parents were missionaries, and we lived in a small village in which we were the only foreigners. The closest expatriates were a half-hour drive away! In my first school I was the only non-Egyptian. So I grew up knowing what it is like to be alone, different, a foreigner in an alien land.

The attitude of my family toward our host nation always was that we were guests and needed to be sensitive to the laws and social mores of the land. Our permit to live in Egypt had to be renewed periodically, and there was no guarantee we could stay. As the 1967 war was about to begin, we were forced to leave on short notice with only a suitcase, and we became refugees in Cyprus where we lived in tents for two months. My parents never returned to Egypt, and as a family we never saw our possessions left in Egypt again, except for a few items.

Fortunately I have been to Egypt regularly since the 1970s, and for the past ten years I have been directing an archaeological excavation in Sinai, Egypt (see my website, www.tellelborg.org). Regularly I talk with friends in Egypt who want to immigrate to the USA, Canada, or Australia. They ask for advice, and they tell me of the endless process involved in getting the needed documentation to move to a new country. I have also had friends who were denied visitor's visas to the West. What especially galls immigrants (and those whose applications are in progress) who go through the legal requirements to become immigrants in America is when people do not follow the rules. They think it is unjust that while they go through the legal process that can take years, many foreigners enter or stay in a country illegally and benefit from their illegality, being employed, getting social and medical benefits, and seeing their children getting free public education.

I am keenly aware of the challenges that immigrants face in a new land. I know of this firsthand from my wife's family and parents, Alfred and Miriam Tom, in whose memory this book is dedicated. They were Chinese Americans who worked hard and sacrificed so their three children could receive a college education, a privilege they themselves could not afford when they graduated from high school. My wife and I have two children who are of mixed race, and our daughter married a first-generation immigrant from the Philippines.

It goes without saying that because I have been a refugee and an alien in two countries, and I am married to a woman of Chinese heritage who is the granddaughter of immigrants, I am sensitive to the plight of immigrants. As one who daily watches the news on TV, listens to it on the radio, and reads press reports, I have closely followed the immigration debate in America.

At the same time, I have been teaching Bible, particularly Old Testament, in colleges and for the past decade at a seminary. I was aware that many characters in the pages of the Bible were immigrants and that a significant number of laws in the legal code dealt with aliens. Given the national debate on immigration that has been ongoing in America for some years now and has spilled over into the church, I was surprised that little serious study of relevant biblical data has occurred that might address the ethical and legal questions surrounding the illegal immigrant. In the final stages of writing this book, I learned of a book by M. Daniel Carroll R., another Old Testament professor, from Denver Seminary, *Christians on the Border* (Baker Academic, 2008), that covers some of the same Scriptures and issues that I do in this book. Carroll takes a slightly different approach than I do. My book is not intended to be a response to *Christians on the Border* as it was nearly complete when I saw Carroll's book. I will, however, address some points of departure. Readers are encouraged to carefully read both books and decide for themselves how best to integrate the teachings of Scripture with current immigration problems.

What I have attempted to do in this book is to take a comprehensive look at the Bible to see how it directly and indirectly tackles the issues surrounding aliens or immigrants. I have made every effort to understand the biblical passages in their historical and cultural context and to consider these through the lens of Christian ethics and the theological affirmation that immigrants are people made in the image of God. Then I attempt to look at the role that law plays and the obligation of citizens in general and Christians in particular, not to mention immigrants, to the rule of law.

Throughout the book I frequently quote the Bible passages under study so that the reader can see the text under discussion. These passages will be from the New International Version unless otherwise stated. Hopefully by examining critical texts and discussing their contextual meaning, light will be shed on the pressing issues faced by this nation and its churches.

I am grateful to the editors at Crossway for their professionalism in the production of this book, especially Ted Griffin, Justin Taylor, and Allan Fisher.

chapter 1

# CRISIS AT THE BORDER

You only need to turn on the news to realize that we have a problem. Some might even label it a crisis. It is not just an American issue—illegal immigration has become the major social and legal challenge facing the western world in the twenty-first century. By the middle of 2006, over eight thousand West Africans had sailed in small boats to the Spanish Canary Islands off the coast of Morocco, hoping to settle in Spain.[1] On June 20, 2006, a group of Afghan asylum-seekers took sanctuary in St. Patrick's Cathedral in Dublin and began a hunger strike to draw attention to their demands, threatening suicide if the police tried to remove them. Neighboring Britain believes there are more than a half million illegal immigrants within its borders. And in Germany reports indicate there are more than one million "illegals." Even distant Australia is experiencing what CNN.com called "a tide" of illegal immigrants.

But in America the numbers are even more staggering. An estimated twelve to fifteen million (some reports are as high as twenty million) now reside illegally in the U.S.A. In one border state, Arizona, 10 percent of the population is now made up of illegal aliens.[2] In April and May of 2006, millions of immigrants and their supporters took to the streets of New York, Los Angeles,

[1]As reported in the *International Herald Tribune*, June 2, 2006, 3.
[2]As reported on Fox News, December 12, 2007.

and other American cities to demand the rights of citizens. In the eyes of many, this was a polarizing development because illegal immigrants came out of the shadows in droves to press Congress for legal recognition and to protest a law passed by the House of Representatives that made entering America illegally a felony.

In 2007 the Senate, with the prompting of President George Bush, tried to pass a comprehensive immigration bill that sought a legal solution to the undocumented millions. That summer, however, the measure failed due to an outcry from angry constituents who did not want to give "amnesty" to those who enter America illegally, while others thought that the path to legalization was too severe and would pose excessive financial hardship on poor people. These polar opposite positions indicated just how divided the American people are on the problem of illegal aliens.

This is not the place to debate the problems or the merits of immigration for America. The pressing issue is what to do with the millions of illegal aliens already here. Furthermore, politicians have had a difficult time agreeing on how or whether to defend the southern border, although a consensus has emerged that defending that border is a necessary first step. The world's longest undefended border, that between Canada and the U.S.A., has not been an issue because there has not been an onslaught of illegal entries from the north. Consequently, most of the current debate surrounds the border between the U.S. and Mexico.

While some argue over the economic issues of immigration, that is, whether it is good or bad for the economy, others focus on the moral and legal questions. As a result, the nation as a whole and politicians in particular are divided. Republicans in the House and the Senate support diametrically opposing bills on how to handle the status of illegal immigrants—amnesty versus none. Democrat leaders are less divided, but there are differences among them nonetheless. Similarly, the Christian community is also at odds regarding the proper response to the immigration problem. *Christianity Today* magazine in a recent article offered this gripping subtitle: "Evangelical leaders divided over moral, policy questions on immigration."[3] No doubt people who consider the Bible to be a source of moral and ethical authority want to know what it has to say on how the nation should respond to the presence of illegal immigrants.

We live in times when the clamor to separate church from state has become shrill. Appealing to the Bible to help arbitrate the rather hostile national discourse may not seem like the obvious thing to do at this time in our nation's history. After all, some might appeal to the Bible because they wish to impose "biblical" law on America, an anathema to secularists who represent the opposite extreme and don't want the Bible to have any role in public policy or law. Such objections notwithstanding, the reality is that various communities, human rights organizations, and churches are appealing to teachings, laws, principles, and practices from the Bible or are quoting Scripture as the basis for the positions they advocate regarding immigration and the treatment of illegal aliens.

As already mentioned, some churches offer sanctuary to illegal aliens within their walls, and some individuals occupy churches in hopes of obtaining asylum. One well-publicized case in the U.S. was that of Elvira Arellano, a woman who had been ordered deported by a judge because of her undocumented status. Along with her son who was born in the U.S.A., she took sanctuary in a Methodist church in Chicago for a year. The pastor of Adalberto United Methodist Church, Rev. Walter Coleman, posted a lengthy statement on the church website condemning American immigration laws and suggesting that Ms. Arellano's sanctuary was divine protection. He explained that "God has protected Elvira from deportation so that the light of truth and love might come into this debate and replace both the vicious self-degradation of hate and the arrogant self-righteousness of paternalism." In August 2007, however, she emerged from the precinct, was arrested a short time later, and was expatriated. The reaction was telling: some wept, others cheered.

Some city councils—San Francisco, Denver, Minneapolis, New

[3]See http://www.christianitytoday.com/ct/2006/aprilweb-only/115-44.0.html.

York, New Haven to name a few—have declared their community to be a "sanctuary city." This means that the city will not cooperate with or assist federal officials who want to arrest and deport aliens. The practice of sanctuary—a place of legal protection—is rooted in laws of the Torah or Old Testament law. Sanctuary is not a modern practice invented to aid illegal immigrants. It goes back over three thousands years! So whether people realize it or not, the Bible is influencing the immigration debate and even inspiring the actions taken by some individuals, organizations, and municipalities. A crucial question must be asked, however: Is the Bible being used correctly by those who offer and practice sanctuary? This matter will be addressed in Chapter 4.

Those who support illegal immigrants on moral grounds, like Christians for Comprehensive Immigration Reform and the Sojourners, appeal to Bible verses like "When a stranger resides with you in your land, you shall not oppress the stranger. The stranger who resides with you shall be to you as the citizen among you. You shall love the stranger as yourself, for you were strangers in the land of Egypt. I am the LORD your God" (Lev. 19:33–34). In fact this verse is posted on their website.[4]

Meanwhile the law-and-order camp appeals to St. Paul's teachings in Romans 13:1: "Everyone must submit himself to the governing authorities"—i.e., the laws of the land. As noted already, the sanctuary movement originates with the practice of taking sanctuary in the cities of refuge as established in the Old Testament law. However, sanctuary advocates seem totally unaware of the conditions prescribed in the Bible for receiving sanctuary protection. Then, too, most Americans simply do not know that the Bible has much to say about immigration and immigrants. Clearly what we need is a fair and balanced treatment of all relevant biblical material to examine how it addresses these issues and to see what wisdom it might offer us. The fact is, the Bible records many stories that deal with immigrants as well as containing many laws and

---

[4]See the Sojourner's website where this verse is quoted on a press release dated 12/17/2007: www.sojo.net/index.cfm?action=action.display&item=CCIR_main.

ethical principles that could guide America, its people, organizations, churches, and even lawmakers as this nation wrestles with one of the most vexing issues of our time.

In this book we shall carefully examine the relevant biblical texts that bear on the issue of immigration and aliens. The narratives and laws of the Bible did not take place in a cultural and historical vacuum. Consequently, we will need to look at other ancient texts from the world of the Bible to understand what was going on during the days of Abraham, Moses, and David that shaped the teaching of Scripture. In my view this contextual approach is essential for establishing the setting of biblical stories and laws, thus providing the basis for understanding them.

Migrations of peoples did not begin with the Americas in the early seventeenth century. They have been a part of human history since God expelled Adam and Eve from the Garden of Eden and they settled east of Eden (Gen. 3:22–24). When Cain murdered his brother Abel, he went in search of a new home, fearing that someone would avenge the death of Abel. So he immigrated to the land of Nod ("wandering"), where he built himself a new home (Gen. 4:14–17). From the early pages of Genesis onward, there are reports of families, clans, and tribes migrating to foreign lands. For example, the people who built the tower of Babel (Gen. 11:1ff.) had emigrated from the east and settled in the land of Shinar, present-day Iraq. Centuries later, Abraham and his family migrated from the same region to the land of Canaan (Gen. 11:31–12:9), and this is where the story of ancient Israel's ancestors begins.

What can we learn from these stories? What do the biblical laws dealing with immigration say regarding the alien that could help us today? On the one hand they protect the immigrant, while on the other hand they safeguard the nation receiving the new aliens.

In the following chapters we shall look at the biblical stories and laws, while at the same time we must consider their cultural, social, and legal settings in order to glean information about how ancient peoples dealt with the age-old quandary of immigration and aliens. The intended result is that readers will have a handle for opening the Bible and using it in a responsible way when considering the policies toward and treatment of aliens and illegal immigrants in America. Of course, the issues treated here will be germane to citizens of any nation who have to face these issues and are looking for some direction on one of the most complex ethical dilemmas of our time.

*Warning!* When I began thinking about this issue, I thought an easy answer would emerge—a single verse or teaching, a silver bullet to solve the problem once and for all. Well, it is not that easy. I was pleased to discover that the Bible goes further than I had expected to address some of the issues we face regarding immigration. It is also clear that Scripture can critique misguided positions that some people have taken. Furthermore, it clarified some questions I had not expected it to address, such as what constituted an alien and the circumstances under which one could settle in a different country. The passages we will consider have something to say to the judicial system, to religious and political leaders, to employers, and to immigrants, legal and illegal. These do not offer a simple answer to our thorny problems, but they do provide some helpful guidelines that can inform the debate and perhaps move the national discourse in a constructive direction.

## APPLYING THE BIBLE TO PRESENT-DAY LAWS AND ISSUES

How do we apply biblical law to current issues? How do we apply the ancient Hebrew prophets' call for justice in Israel to contemporary western societies? These questions must be thoughtfully considered because the hermeneutical issues are thorny. Four common approaches will be considered here.

One way of applying biblical law to modern issues and laws is to look for literal correlations between the two. While this way of viewing the Bible is common among very conservative readers of Scripture, this approach is seriously flawed. I think most readers of the Old Testament law, Christians or Jews, will agree that the Sinai legislation of Exodus 20–Deuteronomy 34 constituted the legal code for Israel and not for the U.S.A, Canada, the European Union, or any other country, although Christians will affirm with the apostle Paul that the Hebrew Scriptures were "written down for our instruction" (1 Cor. 10:11, ESV) and that God's word "remains forever" (Isa. 40:8; 1 Pet. 1:25), while at the same time concurring with the distinguished theologian Gerhard von Rad that Scripture is "the particular word relevant to a particular hour in history."[5] Consequently we must be very careful about literally applying ancient Israelite law to the present without fully understanding the setting and context of the passage in question.

First, we must recognize the vast differences that exist between the cultural, economic, and social milieu of ancient Israel three thousand years ago and present western culture. They are not the same, and it is misguided to make one-to-one, literal correlations. For example, a person considered poor by modern western standards would be viewed as very affluent in ancient Near Eastern economies. A poor person in America may not have medical insurance (although he or she may have Medicaid or access to public clinics), but the commoner in ancient Israel (most people were farmers or pastoralists) most likely never saw a doctor in his entire life, and his children neither had checkups nor received inoculations! The same is true when we go from those considered to be impoverished in western nations to the poor in parts of Asia or Africa today. So applying ancient biblical law and the prophet's message to the modern western context is not a simple task.

A second approach to applying the Bible to current practices is to take seriously the demand for justice found in Israel's prophets. This appeal is taken by some as a call to fairly apply and practice American law. Martin Luther King Jr., in fact, did this. In his "I Have a Dream" speech, Dr. King quoted Amos—"let justice roll down"—followed by an appeal to the Declaration of Independence when it refers to "unalienable Rights" and "Life, Liberty and the

[5]Gerhard von Rad, *Old Testament Theology*, II (Philadelphia: Westminster Press, 1962), 129.

pursuit of Happiness."[6] He rightly pleaded that blacks were not benefiting from the "Rights" guaranteed in the Constitution. Certainly any fair-minded person will agree that the laws of any nation should be consistently and fairly applied to its population.

A third approach is to examine the legal material in the Torah in order to understand the theological or ethical principle behind the Law and use that doctrine to shape or critique federal, state, and local laws. A proponent of this approach is Walter Kaiser Jr.[7] In this model one examines biblical injunctions as a standard and extracts the ethical principle at work in the Torah. Armed with the ethical teaching, one can then assess present-day statutes and legal precedents to correct or adjust the law, and where there are gaps in our laws, biblical law can offer ethical principles and moral guidelines for establishing new laws.

A fourth method insists that one take a more comprehensive view of the teaching of the Bible in theological, social, and economic areas and thereby establish a biblical worldview as a way of evaluating contemporary social and legal issues. A champion of this approach is Christopher Wright.[8] The advantage to this approach is that one can "preserve the objective" of the biblical teaching "but change the context" to any culture or time.[9] Thus we are not time-bound as in the first approach.

The literal, proof-texting method of the first approach should be avoided because it is simplistic and naive. Typically those who want to apply biblical law to the western context do so selectively, accepting laws they personally feel comfortable with and rejecting those that create unease. The second approach of only using the call for justice in the Bible to promote "American" or "Canadian" justice certainly has much to commend to a society where the laws themselves are generally equitable but are being ignored for whatever reason. Limiting "justice," however, to the application of existing law fails to recognize that the Bible can also serve as

[6]For a copy of this speech, see http://www.americanrhetoric.com/speeches/mlkihaveadream.htm.
[7]Walter Kaiser Jr., *Toward Old Testament Ethics* (Grand Rapids, MI: Baker, 1983).
[8]Christopher Wright, *Walking in the Ways of the Lord: The Ethical Authority of the Old Testament* (Downers Grove, IL: InterVarsity Press, 1995).
[9]Ibid., 114–116.

a moral sounding board for our laws and can serve as an ethical foundation to challenge immoral laws. Certainly we should take the call to justice (social or otherwise) seriously (i.e., apply existing laws), but we must go beyond that.

Where relevant, ethical, and moral principles in biblical law and the application of it by Israel's prophets can serve as a standard by which to evaluate present-day laws, and where the Law is silent, one can employ theological principles in the Bible to shape new laws in a way that would, in the words of the preamble to the American Constitution, "establish Justice, insure domestic Tranquility, provide for the common defence, promote the general Welfare, and secure the Blessings of Liberty." This is the contribution that the system promoted by Kaiser can make. What do we do, then, if the Bible is silent on an issue? For example, the Bible does not mention abortion at all as it was not an issue to ancient Israel. One can indeed make a very strong case against taking life in the womb, but this requires an all-embracing biblical and theological argument.[10]

Wright's model allows one to look for ethical principles in the Bible. However, it is done in a more comprehensive manner by examining the entire canon of Scripture through the lens of the major biblical themes of creation, fall, redemption, and new creation.[11] In the following chapters we shall attempt to use this comprehensive approach especially as it relates to the alien in ancient Israel and then see how it might be relevant to the present dilemma facing people who care about national laws and biblical justice too.

[10]For an example see the author's essay "Abortion and the Old Testament Law," in *Abortion: A Christian Understanding and Response*, ed. James K. Hoffmeier (Grand Rapids, MI: Baker, 1987), 49–63.
[11]Wright, *Walking in the Ways of the Lord*, 14–21.

chapter 2

# IMMIGRATION AND IMMIGRANTS IN ABRAHAM'S WORLD

**Now the LORD said to Abram, "Go from your country and your kindred and your father's house to the land that I will show you." (Gen. 12:1, ESV)**

The story of the people of Israel began with a journey, a long trek from southern Mesopotamia (present-day Iraq), north through Syria, and south to Canaan (present-day Israel). They were immigrants passing through lands not their own along with their flocks and herds. One might think that people could just move about wherever they wanted in ancient times, roam at will, and set up camps freely. This is not an accurate picture, however.

Three and four thousand years ago there were large kingdoms, like those of Egypt, the Hittites of northern Anatolia (present-day Turkey), Assyria, Babylonia, and Persia. Even in ancient times there were clearly delineated lands or countries, some large and others tiny. This is why the Old Testament speaks of the border of the land of Canaan (Exod. 16:35), Egypt (1 Kings 4:21; 2 Chron. 9:26; 26:8), and the borders of Israel (1 Sam. 27:1). From the era of Abraham to the days of Joshua when Israel settled in the land of Canaan, the so-called "Promised Land," that land was made of small city-states whose rulers were called kings despite the limited size of their territory.

Israel's borders are given at different times and places in the Bible, sometimes in general terms, sometimes in great detail. For example, when the land is first promised to Abraham, it is presented in broad strokes from north to south: "from the river of Egypt[1] unto the great river, the river Euphrates" (Gen. 15:18). In Joshua's day, however, when the twelve territories are divided up among the Israelite tribes, each territory within Israel is described in incredible detail, occupying seven chapters in the book of Joshua (13–19).

**FIGURE 1**

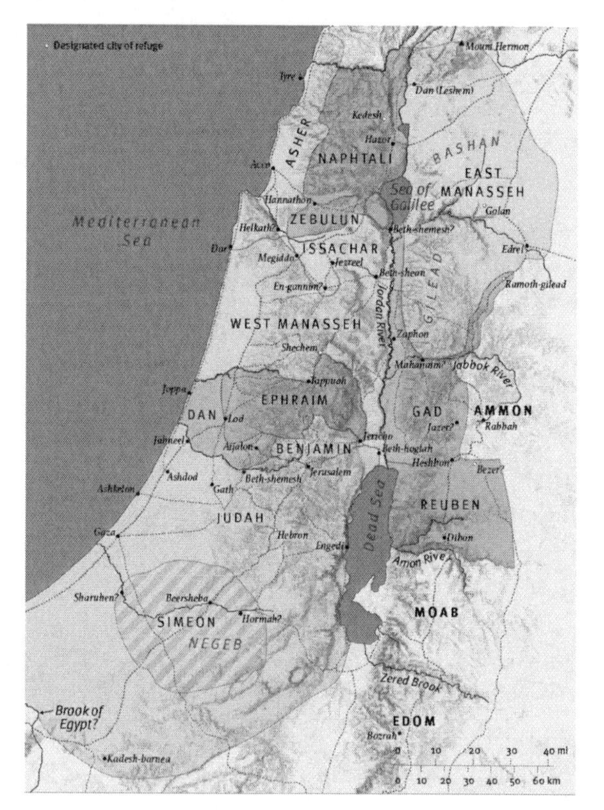


Map of the Promised Land showing allotment of the twelve tribes.

[1]The River of Egypt is not the Nile but is thought to be Wadi El-Arish, a seasonal stream that flows from north-central Sinai to the Mediterranean near modern El-Arish.

Then, too, small nations east of the Jordan River (which demarcated Israel from those territories), opposite Israel, had definite boundaries. In the days of Moses, Edom's northern boundary was the Zered Brook that separated it from Moab (Num. 21:11–12), whose northern border was marked by the Arnon River (Num. 21:13), while farther to the north, the land of the Ammonites began at the Jabbok River (Num. 21:24; see Figure 2). As is the case today, nations and states within a country often use natural borders such as rivers, valleys, and mountain ranges to designate territorial ownership.

**FIGURE 2**

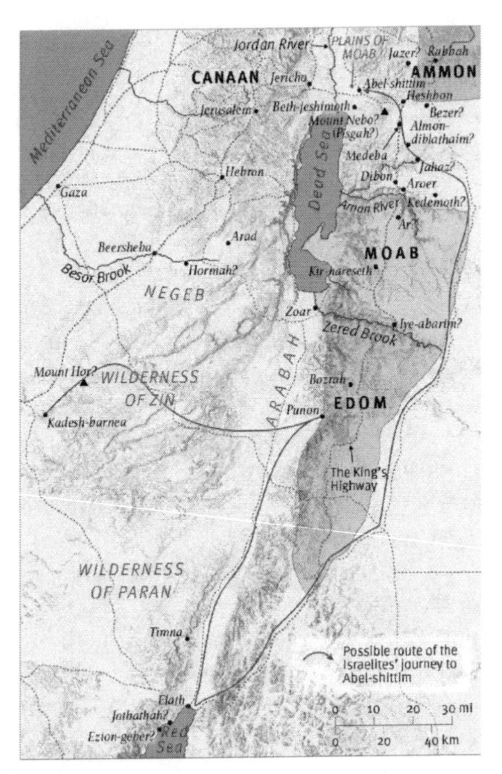


Map of Canaan before the days of Joshua that shows Moab, Ammon, and Edom, and king's highway in Trans-Jordan.

The obvious question is, were ancient territorial borders taken seriously and was national sovereignty recognized? The answer is emphatically *yes*. Not only were wars fought to establish and settle border disputes, borders were vigorously defended, and battles occurred when a neighboring state violated another's territory. So national boundaries were normally honored.

A good illustration of this respect for a nation's territory is recorded in the book of Numbers when Moses and the Israelites, after the exodus from Egypt, wanted to travel from Sinai (a region no one nation completely controlled politically or militarily) and pass through Edom. There an interesting encounter occurred. From Kadesh Barnea, just south of the border of Canaan and with Edom to the east, Moses dispatched messengers to Edom's king with the following request:

> "Now we are here at Kadesh, a town on the edge of your territory. *Please let us pass through your country.* We will not go through any field or vineyard, or drink water from any well. We will travel along the king's highway and not turn to the right or to the left until we have passed through your territory."
>
> But Edom answered: "You may not pass through here; if you try, we will march out and attack you with the sword."
>
> The Israelites replied: "We will go along the main road, and if we or our livestock drink any of your water, we will pay for it. We only want to pass through on foot—nothing else."
>
> Again they answered: "You may not pass through."
>
> Then Edom came out against them with a large and powerful army. Since Edom refused to let them go through their territory, Israel turned away from them. (Num. 20:16–21)

From this episode we can see that the Edomites controlled the strategic north-south road known as the king's highway[2] (see Figure 2) and would not even allow Israel to travel on it through their territory, even though Moses offered to pay a toll! This rejection is out of keeping with the socially accepted custom of offering

[2]This route ran from the Red Sea port of Eloth (Eilat) through Jordan and north to Damascus in Syria.

hospitality to travelers in the ancient and modern Middle East.[3] It is worth noting that even a traveler, a foreigner, passing through the territory of another had to obtain permission to do so.

This was a bitter pill for Israel to swallow, and this snub was recalled over a century later by the judge Jephthah. He also refers to other denials of passage that Moses and the Israelites experienced on the journey to the Promised Land. During his dispute over territory with Israel's neighbors, the Ammonites, that judge declared:

> But when they came up out of Egypt, Israel went through the wilderness to the Red Sea and on to Kadesh. Then Israel sent messengers to the king of Edom, saying, "Give us permission to go through your country," but the king of Edom would not listen. They sent also to the king of Moab, and he refused. So Israel stayed at Kadesh.
>
> Next they traveled through the wilderness, skirted the lands of Edom and Moab, passed along the eastern side of the country of Moab, and camped on the other side of the Arnon. They did not enter the territory of Moab, for the Arnon was its border.
>
> Then Israel sent messengers to Sihon king of the Amorites, who ruled in Heshbon, and said to him, "Let us pass through your country to our own place." Sihon, however, did not trust Israel to pass through his territory. He mustered all his army and encamped at Jahaz and fought with Israel. (Judg. 11:16–20)

These episodes demonstrate clearly that nations could and did control their borders and determined who could pass through their land.

On the individual, family, and clan level, property was owned and boundaries established. Personal property and fields were delineated by landmarks, stone markers of some sort. For this reason, the Mosaic Law prohibited the removal of landmarks (Deut. 19:14), and an even stronger denunciation is made in Deuteronomy 27:17: "Cursed is the man who moves his neighbor's boundary

[3]On the practice of hospitality in Bible times, see Victor H. Matthews and Don C. Benjamin, *Social World of Ancient Israel 1250–587 BCE* (Peabody, MA: Hendrickson, 1993), Chapter 6.

stone." During the period of the divided kingdom (eighth century B.C.), the prophet Hosea decried the leaders of Judah for seizing the territory of her sister kingdom Israel by taking their boundary stones. Removing either a nation's or an individual's landmarks was not merely encroaching upon one's land—it was ultimately robbery. Theft is associated with moving boundary stones by the sage Job (Job 24:2).

Both in Israel and elsewhere in the biblical world, purchasing and owning property was a legal matter that typically entailed drafting a legal contract that was witnessed at the time of the transaction. And within Israel, land was always to be kept within the family or clan.

Genesis offers a detailed report of Abraham's purchase of property for the burial of his wife, Sarah (more on this below). It occurred in the gate of the city of Hebron (Gen. 23:10). The gate area of the city was where official and legal matters were conducted, and in the case of purchasing land, the price was negotiated publicly. More information about the purchase of land is given in the book of Jeremiah when the prophet buys land from his cousin in keeping with the principle that property should never be sold outside of one's clan or tribe (Lev. 25:23–28). The price was recorded, and then the prophet announced, "I signed and sealed the deed, had it witnessed, and weighed out the silver on the scales" (Jer. 32:10). There were two copies of the deed, one sealed and the other left open (v. 11). Witnesses also signed the documents. The sealed document was not just a backup; rather, should anyone dispute details of the open deed or accuse the owner of amending the contract, the sealed copy could be opened to prove what was recorded in the original one.

These episodes illustrate that on the personal or family level, property was legally owned and purchased. Deeds existed to prove ownership, and as noted above, landmarks plainly identified one's property. The practice of having two deeds shows that ownership was a serious, legal matter. Above all, one's property should be respected.

As mentioned above, organized kingdoms had clearly established borders and often had forts and military patrols to protect their land from hostile invasion and uncontrolled migrations. In some cases defenses were hastily built to inhibit mass movements of peoples. Just before 2000 B.C. there was a major ethnic movement of Amorites, a Semitic-speaking people from northern Syria. They infiltrated the Tigris-Euphrates valley into Sumer in southern Mesopotamia. The Sumerian rulers in southern Mesopotamia tried in vain to forestall this movement. Records show that in his fourth year King Shu-Sin built a series of forts or walls to keep away the Amorites.[4] Shu-Sin was King of Ur in southern Iraq, which at that time was the dominant city and capital of Sumer. In subsequent years the infiltrations continued, and the Amorites eventually overwhelmed Sumerian defenses, took control of cities, and in time Sumerian language, religion, culture, and traditions were replaced by those of the Amorites. One of their chieftains is credited with founding the city of Babylon, and from there his successors ruled. One in particular distinguished himself as a great conqueror and lawgiver, the legendary Hammurabi who reigned around 1792–1750 B.C.

Indeed many of the mass migrations throughout history have resulted in the eclipsing of various languages, cultures, and the national sovereignty of countries.

## ABRAHAM THE IMMIGRANT

The Bible traces Israel's origin back to Abraham. He traveled with his father Terah and the extended family from Ur of the Chaldees to Haran according to Genesis 11:31, a distance of about five hundred miles.[5] Ur was the impressive ancient Sumerian city-state of southern Mesopotamia whose history can be traced back to the fifth millennium B.C. Why this family left that glorious city with its

---

[4]Georges Roux, *Ancient Iraq* (Baltimore: Penguin, 1969), 160–161.

[5]Some theorize that there was another site named Ur located in northern Mesopotamia nearer to Haran and that this was Abraham's original home. See Barry Bietzel, *Moody Atlas of Bible Lands* (Chicago: Moody, 1985), 80–81. However, the majority of biblical scholars and historical geographers prefer Ur in Sumer.

advanced culture is not disclosed in Genesis. The clan trekked to Haran in northern Mesopotamia where they settled, although the land of Canaan was the original destination (see Figure 3). Why the journey was interrupted at Haran is not reported. The distance from Haran to Canaan was yet another four hundred miles. Clearly these were excruciatingly long and demanding migrations. Given the fact that Terah, his sons, and the wives whose names we know are of Northwest Semitic type and had lived in Ur suggests that their ethnicity was not Sumerian but Amorite.[6] This consideration may offer a clue as to why they put roots down in Haran (Gen. 11:31), which was in the region from which the Amorites originated.

**FIGURE 3**

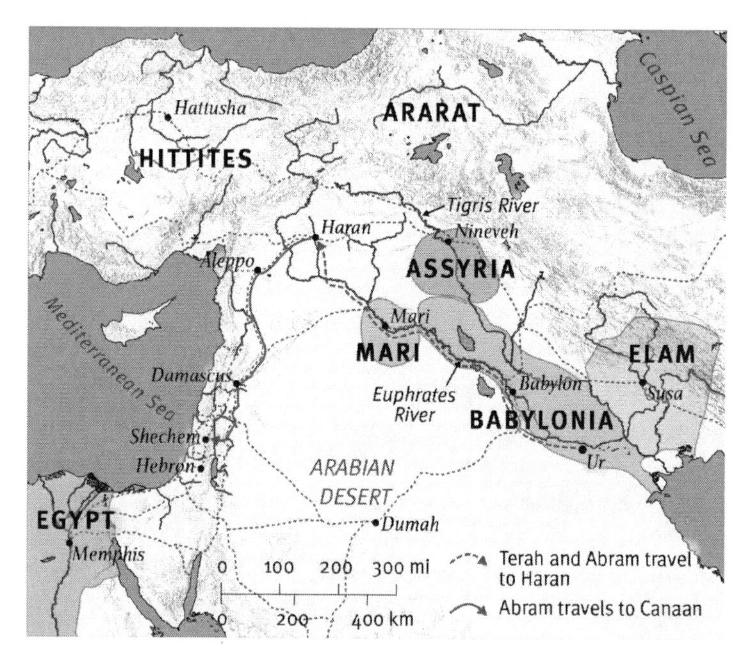


Map of Ancient Near East showing Abraham's journeys.

[6]Kenneth A. Kitchen, *The Reliability of the Old Testament* (Grand Rapids, MI: Eerdmans, 2003), 341–343.

Ancient Haran has been discovered by archaeologists and is located in present-day Turkey just north of the Syrian border. Its name means "crossroads" as it was situated at a key point with routes coming from southern Mesopotamia, northward to ancient Hatti in central Turkey, and southeast to Aram (Syria), Phoenicia (Lebanon), and Canaan/Israel. Based on ancient texts, we know that it was on a well–traveled trade route between Sumer and the Levant, or the area of Lebanon and Israel.[7] Could it be that Terah's decision to migrate from southern Mesopotamia was because he or his forebears had been part of the southward Amorite movement? The original plan to relocate to Canaan may have been because it too was home to other Amorite tribes that had moved southwest into Canaan and the Trans-Jordan (i.e., modern Jordan). The Bible does report that there were Amorites in the land in Abraham's day (Gen. 10:16; 14:7; 15:16, 21).

Genesis 11:32 explains that Terah died in Haran, which might indicate that age or health issues figured in the settling down in the area the Bible calls Naharaim (i.e., "the two rivers," the Euphrates and Tigris, giving rise to the Greek name Mesopotamia).

After the announcement of Terah's death, the narrative indicates that God directed Abraham to leave his new home and go to the land he would give him (Gen. 12:1–3). Armed with promises of divine blessings and a land—hence the expression "the Promised Land"—Abraham headed off to Canaan. Thus he completed the journey his father and the rest of the family had earlier set out to achieve. But there was a problem for Abraham, his wife Sarah, and his nephew Lot and their considerable flocks, herds, and cattle. Genesis 12:6 reveals that "Abram traveled through the land. . . . At that time the Canaanites were in the land." Not only was Abraham a foreigner in an alien land, but he was surrounded by a Canaanite majority. The Canaanites were another Semitic-speaking people with whom he could have easily communicated.

In Canaan Abraham identifies himself to the Hittites[8] of Hebron

---

[7]For a map that shows the trade and travel routes in the early part of the second millennium B.C., see W. W. Hallo and W. K. Simpson, *The Ancient Near East: A History* (New York: Harcourt Brace Jovanovich, 1971), 90–91.

[8]The identity of the Hittites in Genesis 23 is a matter of scholarly debate. Some think they are

as a sojourner or alien (*ger*, Genesis 23:40), a person (or family) who resides, temporarily or permanently, outside his or her homeland. Later on we will examine this critical term, and we will see that it applies to the Israelites when they live in Egypt and subsequently to foreigners who reside with the Israelites (see next section).

Like other pastoral nomads, Abraham moved from the cooler climes of the hill country in central Canaan to the dry regions of the south—Shechem, Bethel, Ai, and the Negev are named (Gen. 12:6–9). The Negev today remains home to tent-dwelling Arab shepherds despite its generally dry desert-like terrain. A drought and the resulting famine prompted Abraham to seek refuge in the well-watered Nile Valley (Gen. 12:10). This ill-fated trip to Egypt is instructive on how foreign immigrants were treated in Pharaonic Egypt, and information from Egypt in turn provides valuable background information on Abraham's brief visit and the later Israelite sojourn in Egypt.

## IMMIGRANTS AND FOREIGNERS IN ANCIENT EGYPT

Throughout most of the second millennium B.C. when the events of Genesis likely occurred, Egypt was fabulously wealthy in material riches like gold, fresh water, and verdant fields. To those who eked out a living by sheepherding in southern Canaan, the Trans-Jordan, and Sinai, Egypt was the land of opportunity not unlike America to millions today. Consequently, over the millennia foreign pastoralists visited Egypt especially during times of famine, economic hardship, and political upheaval. Egyptian texts bear witness to this reality, and they display antipathy toward wandering Semites (i.e., pastoral nomads). This aversion is reflected in the Joseph narrative when the other sons of Jacob come to Egypt and we are informed, "for all shepherds are detestable to the Egyptians" (Gen. 46:34). Consequently, the Egyptians were very careful about who was admitted and why.

A celebrated tomb scene from a governor of middle Egypt during

---

related to the Indo-European people by the same name who lived in central Anatolia, present-day Turkey. Others consider them also to be a Semitic-speaking group like the Canaanites.

the nineteenth century B.C. shows a band of Semites entering his territory (Figure 4). The leader's name is given in hieroglyphics as Abishai, which is Northwest Semitic, and he bears the title "foreign chieftain." He is followed by men, women, children, and donkeys that bear their gear. Their hairstyles, beards, and clothes contrast with those of the Egyptians in the same painting, revealing their different ethnicity and foreign status. In front of the chief an Egyptian official presents their credentials, the Egyptian equivalent to a visa authorizing them to be there, either for work, possibly as blacksmiths (two sets of bellows are included on the pack animals) or more likely as miners in search of galena.[9] Evidently economic opportunity brought these workers to central Egypt. However they had a permit that allowed this band of thirty-seven to enter and work. The document is displayed in the scene in such a way that one can read its contents (see Figure 5). It is dated to the sixth year of Pharaoh Senusert II, or 1862 B.C., and records the number of Semites for which the visa applies.

**FIGURE 4**

Semites entering Egypt in ca. 1860 B.C. for employment purposes.

[9]The accompanying inscription mentions that they were bringing galena (the Egyptian word is *msdnt*).

**FIGURE 5**

Detail of the permit for entry into this part of Egypt. It specifies that there are 37 Asiatics in the group.

From this same period, texts shed further light on the Egyptian attitude toward foreigners in general and immigrants in particular. In the Wisdom for Merikare from around 2200 B.C., King Khety tells of his strategy to deal with infiltrating pastoralists several centuries before Abraham's time. He claims to have populated the northeastern delta "in order to repulse barbarians." He then describes the lot of these intruders: "as for the miserable Asiatic,[10] wretched is the place where he is; lacking in water, hidden because of trees. . . . He does not settle in one place. Food causes his feet to

[10]The term used is Aamu, a generic term used by the Egyptians for the Semitic-speaking people of west Asia or the area of present-day Israel, Lebanon, and Syria.

roam."[11] The southern part of Canaan is described here as undesirable with insufficient water and food, which propels them to come to Egypt for sustenance. This same land that served as a spawning ground for immigrants trying to get into Egypt is the same territory where Abraham, Isaac, and Jacob grazed their flocks in the book of Genesis. From here Abraham and Jacob both launched trips to Egypt.

Another informative piece of Egyptian literature is the Prophecy of Neferti that dates to around 1960 B.C. It describes the sorry state of Egypt in the previous chaotic epoch. Because of the lack of a strong king, Egypt's frontier forts were not manned with soldiers, which allowed foreigners to infiltrate unchecked into the land and settle in the Delta. He then announces that a future king (whose name he predicts as Ameny, short for Amenemhet) would reverse Egypt's fortunes and "build the 'Walls of the Ruler' . . . to prevent Asiatics from going down into Egypt. They [will have to] beg for water in the customary manner in order to let their flocks drink."[12] This last line reminds us again that the principal reason why people from ancient Canaan came to Egypt was to find water for their flocks and that the Egyptian border forts were intended to control their movements and prevent unauthorized infiltration. With the forts occupied, Neferti observes, the foreigners will have to come and beg for water, that is, get permission for access to Egyptian water sources rather than just penetrating Egypt's frontier at will and with impunity as they had during Egypt's period of political and military weakness when the border forts were not manned with troops.

A communiqué from a frontier fort commander to his superior back in the capital from the end of the thirteenth century B.C. offers some additional insights into how the Egyptians handled pastoral nomads who came in search of water. The officer reports that he granted passage to a band of Edomite Bedouin and their flocks so they could enter the area of Tjeku (Succoth of the Bible) to the Pools of Pithom. This is the present-day Wadi Tumilat, west of Ismailiya. In

---

[11]Translation in James K. Hoffmeier, *Israel in Egypt: The Evidence for the Authenticity of the Exodus Tradition* (New York: Oxford, 1999), 55.
[12]Ibid., 59.

ancient times this was one of the main means of access to and egress from Egypt. A humanitarian touch is evident. The border guard gave these needy people access to water but did not allow them to freely roam and likely put a time limit on their stay in Egypt.

The Brooklyn Museum houses a papyrus from about 1750 B.C. that records the names of around forty foreigners who worked on the estate of an upper-class landowner in Egypt (Figure 6).[13] We know they are foreigners because they have Semitic names like Aper-Reshep, Menahem, and Shiprah, coupled with the hieroglyph for "Semitic-foreigner." Some of the jobs they did included weaving and being household servants. While many people entered Egypt as low-skilled laborers, others were artisans. The circumstances under which they came to Egypt are not known. Perhaps some, like Joseph, were brought as slaves, and in time most assimilated into Egyptian society.

**FIGURE 6**

Papyrus Brooklyn, 35.1446 includes the names of Semitic-speaking slaves in Egypt around 1862 B.C.

[13]William C. Hayes, *A Papyrus of the Late Middle Kingdom in the Brooklyn Museum* (Brooklyn: The Brooklyn Museum, 1955), 92–98.

Clearly the Egyptians were not anti-immigration or against foreigners per se (an impression you might get from reading the early chapters of Exodus), but they did want their sovereignty respected and their borders protected, and they wanted to control who entered their land and why. It is fair to say that this is the attitude of most countries today.

To protect their territorial integrity, the Egyptians built border forts throughout much of the second millennium B.C. to protect against hostile invasions and mass migrations and even to monitor smaller immigrant groups. Mention has been made of Pharaoh Amenemhet I (1961–1943 B.C.) who built The Walls of the Ruler to keep out Asiatic Bedouins. At the two main entry points into Egypt from Sinai, special *khetem*-forts were situated to monitor people, and documents may have been sealed or stamped as the word *khetem* suggests.

**FIGURE 7a**

Wall of frontier fort (ca. 1300–1200 B.C.) from Tel el-Borg, N. Sinai.

Egypt's main northeastern entry point was only discovered in the 1980s in North Sinai at a site called Tell Hebua.[14] There is evidence that it was occupied as early as the beginning of the second millennium B.C., and a massive fortress measuring over 800 by 400 yards long is currently being excavated. Then in 2007 a second fort with forty-feet-thick walls was uncovered at Hebua II less than a mile away from the first fort. This recently discovered fort was the Khetem-fort that was the entry checkpoint to Egypt. Since 1999 I have directed excavations at Tell el-Borg in northwest Sinai. There we have discovered and excavated the remains of two frontier forts just in Sinai, six miles east of the Suez Canal, that defended a strategic area near the border between 1450 and 1200 B.C.[15] (see Figures 7a-b).

**FIGURE 7b**

Fired brick foundation of moat of earlier fort (ca. 1450-1300 B.C.) from Tell el-Borg, N. Sinai.

[14]Mohamed Abd el-Maksoud, *Tell Hebuoa (1981–1991)* (Paris: Éditions Recherche sur les Civilisations, 1998).

[15]See the project's website for pictures and reports: www.tellelborg.org.

South of Egypt was the biblical land of Kush in modern-day Sudan. Kush or Nubia was Egypt's main source of gold throughout Pharaonic times. At the same period as The Walls of the Ruler guarded Egypt's frontier with western Asia, Egypt had extended its hegemony into Nubia (northern Sudan), and more than a dozen forts were constructed along the Nile to protect Egypt's interests in the region (see Figure 8). Pharaoh Senusert III (1862–1843 B.C.) erected a stone slab or stela at one of these forts, the inscription of which made the following claims: "the king made his southern border at Heh" (modern Semna in Sudan). To his successors he declared: "Now my majesty has had an image made of my majesty, at this border which my majesty made, in order that you maintain it, in order that you fight for it."[16]

**FIGURE 8**

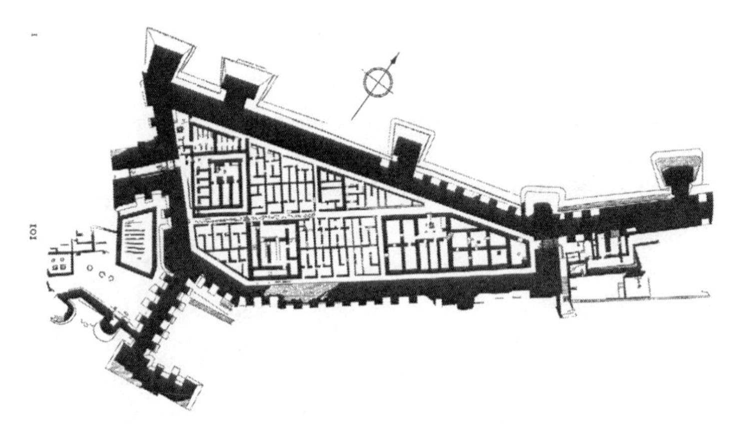

Plan of Nubian fort at Uronarti.

Those who were permitted to enter typically assimilated within several generations and were Egyptianized, although some moved in and out seasonally, especially the pastoralists. Immigrants from western Asia normally retained their Semitic names for a genera-

[16]Miriam Lichtheim, *Ancient Egyptian Literature*, I (Berkeley, CA: University of California Press, 1975), 119–120.

tion or two, and in some cases their careers can be followed in written records. Some advanced socially and professionally. In the 1980s, the French archaeologist Alain-Pierre Zivie discovered the tomb of a high-ranking official from the fourteenth century B.C.[17] His name is Aper-El, which is Semitic, showing that he came from the Levant. We do not know under what circumstances Aper-El came to Egypt or how he was elevated to be a vizier or prime minister who reported directly to the Pharaoh Akhenaten (1352–1336 B.C.). His advancement shows that during New Kingdom times (1540–1070 B.C.), educated and talented foreigners, like Joseph in the book of Genesis two centuries earlier, could be promoted to and held top positions in the administration.

The foregoing data from Egypt provide a number of insights into how the ancient Egyptians dealt with immigrants who wanted to enter the land, as well as the circumstance that Abraham would have faced during his brief stay in Egypt.

## ABRAHAM THE ALIEN

Given what we know about Egypt's attitude and policies toward immigrants during the early second millennium B.C., one might be inclined to think that Abraham too was aware of the problems and possibilities he could encounter in Egypt. "As he was about to enter Egypt" (Gen. 12:11)—perhaps at a border check point?—Abraham does something very odd. Fearing that he might be killed and his beautiful wife taken, Abraham asks his wife Sarah to claim that she is his sister, thinking that "it may go well with me because of you" (Gen. 12:11–13, ESV). Sarah was indeed noticed and "taken" into Pharaoh's house (v. 15). The expression to "take a woman" in Hebrew normally means for marriage. I have elsewhere suggested that behind Abraham's ruse was the attempt to establish diplomatic relations with Pharaoh.[18] Marriage between tribes and nations was a well-attested practice in the ancient Near East, as seen in the Bible, as well as in recent times. Solomon's multiple wives (1 Kings 11:1ff.),

---

[17] Alain-Pierre Zivie, *Découverte à Saqqarah: le vizir oublié* (Paris: Seuil, 1990).

[18] James K. Hoffmeier, "The Wives' Tales of Genesis 12, 20, & 26 and the Covenants at Beersheba," *Tyndale Bulletin*, 43.1 (1992), 81–99.

for example, were meant to consolidate relations with allies or subject nations. Similarly, Pharaohs like Thutmose III (1479–1425 B.C.) and Rameses II (1279–1212 B.C.) married many foreign princesses. The latter consummated a union with the daughter of the Hittite emperor with whom he had been at war less than two decades earlier. The marriage came after a peace treaty had been signed.

Similarly, Abraham was apparently trying to find a legally acceptable means of establishing a bond with a king with whom he wanted to make an alliance. Additionally, Abraham sought to change his status from a foreigner to a resident, from outsider to insider. Things did go well with him until the truth was uncovered (Gen. 12:16–18). Pharaoh ordered his immediate deportation and returned Sarah to her embarrassed husband, and Abraham returned to the Negev, southern Canaan (Gen. 12:20; 13:1).

The same thing happened to Abraham (Gen. 20) and his son Isaac (Gen. 26) with Abimelech, the King of Gerar in southern Canaan. The result in both cases was that treaties were subsequently drafted. It is clear from Genesis 26:17–22 that the issue Abraham had earlier negotiated was water rights in Abimelech's domain and that when he died, Isaac had to negotiate a new arrangement with the king, permitting access to Gerar's water sources (Gen. 26:26–34). Once again the immigrants in Canaan, like those entering Egypt, had to obtain permission to enter a ruler's territory and, in this case, graze herds.

Some time after his return from Egypt, Abraham settled "near the great trees of Mamre at Hebron," a town located around twenty-five miles south of Jerusalem. There he "built an altar to the LORD" (Gen. 13:18). This brief report suggests that as an alien, he could practice his religion freely. Some time later when Sarah died, he needed to purchase property for her burial. Here is how he approached the Hittite residents of Hebron:

> Then Abraham rose from beside his dead wife and spoke to the Hittites. He said, "I am *an alien* and *a stranger among you*. Sell me some property for a burial site here so I can bury my dead." (Gen 23:3–4)

Clearly Abraham recognized that he was an immigrant or alien who needed to accommodate to the laws and norms of the land. One commentator has noted that he could not use "local burial facilities without municipal permission, and he cannot acquire land."[19] Abraham's dilemma may explain his deference to the people of Hebron when he bowed to the men with whom he wanted to do business (Gen. 23:7, 12). This story does show his respect for the citizens of Canaan, but his actions also demonstrate that he realized that he, an alien, had to obey their laws and customs. The price he paid, four hundred shekels (about nine pounds) of silver, is thought to be high, although the size of the field is not given. Some commentators think that because Abraham was an alien, he could not normally own property and hence had to pay an excessive amount for the right to purchase land. If this was the case, we see how easily an alien could be exploited. The point is, however, that Abraham the outsider was respectful of the native population and their customs and laws. As a consequence, they cooperated with him, and an amicable solution to Abraham's problem was reached.

## WHAT IS AN ALIEN ACCORDING TO THE BIBLE?

The Hebrew word usually translated "stranger," "alien," or "sojourner" derives from the verb *gwr*, which occurs eighty-one times in the Old Testament. It means "to sojourn" or "to dwell as a stranger, become a refugee."[20] As a noun, *ger* is found eighty-two times in Hebrew. More than 160 occurrences of these words indicate just how common aliens were in ancient Israel's experience.

But what exactly is a *ger*? One source of confusion for readers of the Bible is that English versions differ on how to translate the Hebrew term *ger*. Some translations, especially older ones, render this word as "stranger" (e.g., KJV, NASB, JB), while others prefer "sojourner" (RSV, ESV). The translation "stranger" is problematic as it is a bit archaic and has different connotations today than it did

[19]Nahum Sarna, *Genesis: The JPS Torah Commentary* (Philadelphia: Jewish Publication Society, 1989), 156.
[20]*NIDOTTE*, 1, 836.

in the past. More modern versions opt for the translation "alien" (NEB, NIV, NJB, NRSV). Unfortunately some contemporary versions render *ger* as "foreigner" (TNIV, TLV). "Foreigner" is hardly an adequate alternative as it is too vague, not to mention being misleading because different Hebrew words are rendered "foreigner" in the Bible, *nekhar* and *zar*.[21] In the end, the TNIV and TLV end up translating both words as "foreigner" (cf. Exod. 23:12; Deut. 1:16; 14:21 where *nekhar* is used). The words *ger* and *nekhar* refer to two different categories of people, as we will see below. The two cannot be confused. Understanding the Bible's definition of an alien or sojourner and how one attained that status is critical to the current debate because advocates for illegal immigrants are using passages from the Old Testament to support their position as if the English word *alien* and the Hebrew word *ger* have the exact same meaning.

One advocacy group, Christians for Comprehensive Immigration Reform, on the Sojourners website, quotes Leviticus 19:33, which states "When a stranger [i.e., *ger*] resides with you in your land, you shall not oppress the stranger. The stranger who resides with you shall be to you as the citizen among you," and then based on this Scripture they declare, "we are working together to revive comprehensive immigration reform as soon as possible, because we share a set of common moral and theological principles that compel us to love and care for the stranger among us."[22]

While this compassionate concern is commendable, their statement begs the question, does the word *ger* (i.e., alien, sojourner, stranger) apply to immigrants regardless of their legal standing? If people with varying views on the status of illegal immigrants are going to cite the Bible to legitimize their position, especially passages that specifically deal with "aliens," it is imperative to know what the Hebrew Bible meant by the term *ger*. Let us consider further the biblical evidence, especially that furnished by the book of Genesis.

---

[21]KB, 700.

[22]See www.sojo.net/index.cfm?action=action.display&item=CCIR_main.

From the Bible and ethnographic evidence it is evident that outsiders were able to enter and stay in a foreign land because they were offered hospitality by a host, and one's status as an alien was an extension of that welcome.[23] When Abraham approached the residents of Hebron to purchase a burial plot for his wife Sarah who had just died, he identified himself as "an alien and a stranger" (Gen. 23:4) or "an alien and a settler" (NEB). What are the legal and social implications of this identification?

The word *alien* (*ger*) is sometimes coupled with the term *resident* (*toshav*, literally "one who resides"), the second word Abraham attributes to himself. Rather than translating this expression as "an alien and a stranger," the two terms together likely mean "resident alien."[24] Such individuals or families, a clan or tribe, are those who have essentially taken up permanent residence in a foreign land, as Abraham and his family had done in Hebron with the permission of their host. In fact, the residents of Hebron acknowledged Abraham's status as being one who is "among us" (23:6) rather than viewing him as a foreigner (*nekhar* or *zar*). The distinction between the two is not only that the aliens (*gerim*) have resided with a host nation for a period of time, but that "they have abandoned their homeland for political or economic reasons and sought refuge in another community."[25] In other words, the *ger* regards the land of his sojourning as the new home for a protracted time period, while the foreigner does not.

Typically the foreigner is one who travels through a country or is there for business purposes. As a consequence, as we shall see in Chapter 4, the Law prescribes for aliens certain legal protection as well as social and religious benefits that foreigners (*nekhar* and *zar*) do not get.[26] One of the reasons aliens required "a host or patron" was because they would not be a part of any kinship group and

---

[23]Matthews and Benjamin, *Social World of Ancient Israel*, 82–83.
[24]The technical term for using two terms to convey one idea is *hendiadys*, a Greek expression meaning "one through two." An English example would be black and blue for bruised. Commentators have suggested that in the case of Abraham, a hendiadys is intended; cf. Sarna, *Genesis*, 158.
[25]*NIDOTTE*, 1, 837.
[26]For further discussion, see David Howard Jr., *Joshua: The New American Commentary* (Nashville: Broadman & Holman, 1998), 216.

thus would lack protection.[27] This is why the meaning "protected citizen" can also be applied to the word *ger*.[28] The practice of using a host family or sponsoring individual still persists in some countries to this day for immigrants and refugees.

The alien, then, is a guest of sorts. As such the alien was not entitled to offer hospitality to others. By way of analogy, if one invites guests into one's home, it is hardly appropriate for the visitor to invite other guests into the host's home.

Various Bible stories illustrate that when an alien brought others into the community, it led to the rough treatment of those guests (cf. Gen. 19:1–11; Judg. 19:10–23). Consequently, Matthews and Benjamin, two Bible scholars who specialize in sociological analysis of the Bible, observe that "the right of granting hospitality is reserved to citizens."[29] In other words, the alien could not even open the door to his extended family and relatives to follow their alien family member. (The exception to this rule appears to be that one could marry someone from one's original community, as will be seen below.) As we will see later in this chapter, it is evident that even a high-ranking official like Joseph, an alien in Egypt, had to receive Pharaoh's permission to bring his immediate family to sojourn there.

So the alien was a permanent resident. The foreigner, on the other hand, was not. Two different but virtually synonymous terms are used for foreigner or stranger, *nekhar* and *zar*.[30] In fact, in several passages the terms are used in a parallel manner (Exod. 30:33; Isa. 28:21; Lam. 5:2), showing that they carried a nearly identical meaning. A foreigner could be an invading enemy (*zar*, Isa. 1:7; Obad. 11) or squatters who moved into Israel when the Israelites were removed to Babylon (*nekhar* and *zar*, Lam. 5:2). But for the most part in Israel, foreigners were those who were passing through the land with no intention of taking residence, or perhaps they would be temporarily or seasonally employed. A foreigner could be a trader, merchant, worker, or mercenary. Thus, in the Bible the foreigner and the

[27]Philip J. King and Lawrence E. Stager, *Life in Biblical Israel* (Louisville: Westminster John Knox Press, 2001), 61.
[28]KB, I, 201.
[29]Matthews and Benjamin, *Social World of Ancient Israel*, 84.
[30]*NIDOTTE*, 1, 1142.

alien were *not* the same and should not be confused. Consequently, they had different standing within the community of Israel, socially, legally, and in matters of religion (see Chapter 4).

In the Hebrew Bible the alien (*ger*) was a person who entered Israel and followed legal procedures to obtain recognized standing as a resident alien. Hence I will use the term *alien* or *ger* throughout this book to refer to legal immigrants. Clearly there was a distinction between the alien (*ger*) and a foreigner (*nekhar* or *zar*) in the Old Testament, and this difference will be clear in the narratives, stories, and laws that will be reviewed in the following sections. Additionally, this distinction must be kept in mind when we attempt to apply ethical considerations from the Bible to the present discussions about immigrants.

## THE SOJOURNINGS OF ISAAC AND JACOB

As previously noted, Abraham considered himself a resident alien, that is, a legal permanent resident of the land of Canaan. However, when it came time to marry off his son Isaac, a wife from the old country was preferred. Abraham sternly instructed his servant regarding this matter:

> I want you to swear by the LORD, the God of heaven and the God of earth, that you will not get a wife for my son from the daughters of the Canaanites, among who I am living, but will go to my country and my own relatives and get a wife for my son Isaac. (Gen. 24:3–4)

Marriage always was and remains the key to ethnic assimilation. Genesis teaches that through marriage a man and woman of two different family units become one flesh (2:24). To be of one's flesh and blood is to be family or kin. Jacob's uncle, Laban, warmly received him into his home back in Haran and permitted him to marry his daughters because "you are my own flesh and blood . . . you are a relative of mine" (Gen. 29:14–15). The main reason for seeking a wife within his clan was because Jacob had been urged "not [to] marry a Canaanite woman" (Gen. 28:1). Esau, Jacob's renegade brother, on the other hand, had earlier married two Hittite women, presumably from Hebron, which "were a source of grief to Isaac and Rebekah" (Gen. 26:35). Apparently in an effort to mollify the damage to the family structure, Esau then married a cousin, the daughter of Ishmael, Abraham's son by Hagar (Gen. 28:9).[31]

These stories well illustrate that even in Bible times immigrants often wanted to retain their ethnic "purity" by marrying within their kin-group. Of course, this happens today, especially with first-generation immigrants. Marriage between ethnic groups tends to break down cultural, social, and religious characteristics and distinctions in one party or the other. For Israel, the latter characteristic was paramount. God warned the people through Moses prior to their entry to Canaan after their sojourn in Egypt, "Do not intermarry with them. Do not give your daughters to their sons or take their daughters for your sons, for they will turn your sons away from following me to serve other gods" (Deut. 7:3–4). This prohibition is clearly based on religious or spiritual considerations. Racial bigotry is not the issue (more on this point when we consider the story of Ruth in Chapter 5).

After about twenty years in the Haran area with his mother's family (Gen. 31:41), Jacob returned to Canaan. Subsequently he refers to his two-decade stay in Mesopotamia as a sojourn (*garti*, literally "I sojourned") with Laban (Gen. 32:4). For a period upon his return to Canaan, he settled just outside Shechem (33:18),[32] a town in the hill country, about twenty-five miles north of Jerusalem. There Jacob purchased a lot of undisclosed size for one hundred *kesitahs*[33] from the sons of Hamor (the leading fam-

[31]Another story that illustrates how marriage was viewed as a means of bringing divergent groups together is the horrible story of the rape of Dinah, daughter of Jacob and Leah (Gen. 34). Hamor, father of Shechem, the rapist, offered marriage as the way to ameliorate the situation and unite the two clans (vv. 8–10).

[32]The text literally reads *'et-pᵉneh*—"before" or "in front of" Shechem. Obviously with their sheep, goats, and cattle, they were not residing within the walled city but rather in the surrounding land that belonged to the city-state of Shechem.

[33]This term is different than the shekel used in Abraham's purchase of the field and cave from the residents of Hebron. *Kesitah* actually means "lamb." It might indicate that the purchase price was in sheep, as was the case in ancient Nuzi in northern Mesopotamia where sheep were given in exchange for a grove. In later times Mesha, king of Moab, paid his tribute to Israel in the form of lambs, rams, and wool (2 Kings 3:4). Alternatively, it may be a fixed price the amount of which is unknown.

ily of Shechem) in order to pitch his tents (Gen. 33:19, margin). Once again we see that the Hebrew patriarchs did not presume for themselves the right to live wherever they wanted but had to obtain permission, and then Jacob purchased land.

As the family history of Abraham continues, the focus shifts to Jacob's son Joseph, the spoiled teenager who was gifted in interpreting dreams (Gen. 37:5–11). Throughout the ancient Near East, dreams were considered to be vehicles of divine communication to individuals without the medium of prophets and specialized priests. Out of spite, Joseph's older brothers sold him to merchant traders who in turn took him to Egypt where he was sold to an Egyptian master (Gen. 37:12–28, 36). This episode set the stage for the extended family of Jacob to migrate to Egypt some years later where they would once again be sojourners.

In Egypt, Joseph started out doing menial work for Potiphar, an officer of Pharaoh (Gen. 39:1). When he proved himself to be capable, reliable, and honest, he was promoted to manage the entire estate (Gen. 39:4). It is obvious that within a brief time, Joseph the Hebrew, as he was derisively called by Potiphar's wife (Gen. 39:14), had mastered the Egyptian language so well that when his brothers visited Egypt they did not recognize their brother because he spoke to them in Egyptian and had a translator relay his words to the unsuspecting brothers (Gen. 42:23). Like Aper-el of the fourteenth century B.C., Joseph, a foreigner, a few centuries earlier was promoted to a very high position based on his competence. Joseph was able to assimilate culturally and linguistically without forgetting his mother tongue. He even took an Egyptian name and married an Egyptian woman (Gen. 41:45). Prior to his death, he included in his oral will that he wanted to be buried back in Canaan (Gen. 50:24–25). His request was honored years later when the exodus occurred (Exod. 13:19). A further indication of just how Egyptianized Joseph had become is that when his father Jacob died in Egypt, Joseph ordered him to be mummified, a uniquely Egyptian practice. When Joseph died, he too was mummified, and his remains were placed in a coffin (Gen. 50:26), a patently Egyptian custom, and one not used by Canaanites or Israelites after they settled in the Promised Land.

At the end of the book of Genesis, Jacob's family immigrated to Egypt during a time of famine (Gen. 46–47). Several statements in the narratives are quite instructive, giving us details about the process by which this clan was able to come and sojourn in Egypt.

First, as just noted, Joseph, who already lived in Egypt and was a high-ranking official in the court of Pharaoh, received permission to bring his father Jacob to Egypt along with the rest of the extended family. In fact, Pharaoh offered them the land of Goshen, the most verdant area in the northeastern delta, as a place to graze their flocks and herds (Gen. 45:16–18). Second, upon their arrival in Egypt, Joseph presented his family to his boss (Gen. 47:1–2). Five of the brothers stepped forward with a request: "We have come to live here awhile, because the famine is severe in Canaan and your servants' flocks have no pasture. So now, please let your servants *settle* in Goshen" (47:4). Once again we find that the Hebrew ancestors left one land in which they were sojourning (viz., Canaan) and went to another to sojourn. The phrase "live for awhile" is the verb *gwr*, "sojourn," followed by "settle" or "reside" (*yashav*). Together these two verbs appear as an alternative to the previously discussed idiom *ger wetoshav*, which means "resident alien." This combination of words was found together in Genesis 23 when Abraham described his legal status in Hebron as a legal alien. Now in a new land, and even though invited to live in Egypt by Pharaoh himself, the brothers felt compelled to ask formally for permission to settle as resident aliens with their droves. The king granted their request: "Pharaoh said to Joseph, 'Your father and your brothers have come to you, and the land of Egypt is before you; settle your father and your brothers in the best part of the land'" (47:5–6).

Here also we see that the Hebrew immigrants sought and received permission to enter a foreign land, in this case from the king himself! When the brothers addressed the monarch, not surprisingly they did so showing deference and respect as their request included "please."[34] One can plainly see that Pharaoh asked about their occupation (47:3), and throughout the paragraph of Genesis 47:1–6 there are repeated references to the flocks and herds of the family of Jacob. Evidently the king did not want a group of people entering Egypt to become financially and economically dependent on the governmental resources, as Gordon Wenham cogently observes: "the insistence that they have brought their livestock with them shows that they do not intend to be a burden to the state, but that they do need suitable pastureland."[35] Typically, as is still the practice in the Middle East today, the sheep and goats of pastoralists were welcome into farmers' fields to eat the stubble and roots left after the harvest. With their flocks and herds grazing the rich lands and ample waters of the Delta, the Hebrews were able to live a good life in Egypt.

The arrival of the Hebrews in Egypt for a period of several centuries sets the stage for the book of Exodus, where we find that the welcoming hand that offered a place to sojourn had turned into an oppressive fist. The hard times and enslavement of the Israelite aliens in Egypt provides the ethical basis for the laws that appear in the remainder of the Law or Torah (see Chapter 4).

## OBSERVATIONS ON IMMIGRATION AND ALIENS IN GENESIS

In this chapter we have examined some important narratives regarding Abraham, Isaac, and Jacob in Genesis that provide useful information about immigration and immigrants. Furthermore, we have examined these reports in the light of some contemporary written sources from the biblical world of the second millennium B.C. When we combine this information, we can make the following observations about how foreign immigrants conducted

---

[34]The expression *yeshᵉvu* is the jussive form that is used in making requests: "let us dwell." This form is compounded with the particle *n'a*, which could be rendered as "please" or even "pray, then, let your servants stay. . . ." (NJPS). Its use here shows that Joseph's brothers are being polite, if not deferential.

[35]Gordon Wenham, *Genesis 16–50*, Word Biblical Commentary (Dallas: Word Books, 1994), 445.

themselves, how host nations received them, and the process for becoming a legal alien. Here are some salient points:

1. Immigration was widely practiced in the ancient Near East, and Genesis reflects this reality (e.g., Abraham's travels from Mesopotamia to Syria, Canaan, and Egypt and back to Canaan).
2. National borders and personal property were recognized and respected, even in the case of travelers who wanted to pass through (e.g., Moses and the Israelites were denied passage through the territory of Edom).
3. The Egyptians and Sumerians constructed forts on the frontiers to control their border and to monitor movements of peoples.
4. Immigrants moved considerably but could not just settle wherever they wanted. They would be expelled for violating the laws or mores of a land (e.g., Abraham's expulsion by Pharaoh for lying about the marital status of his wife; Isaac's dismissal from Gerar for the same).
5. Permission was sought by and sometimes granted to immigrants who wanted to settle in another land. (e.g., Abraham in Hebron and Gerar, Isaac in Gerar, Jacob and his family in Egypt).
6. Aliens were not permitted to sponsor other foreigners to receive alien status. Bringing a spouse from the outside seems to be an exception to the rule (e.g., Isaacs's wife Rachel came from northern Syria to Canaan).
7. People were given permits to enter a country for seasonal or periodic employment (e.g., Abishai and his clan as depicted in the Beni Hasan tomb in Egypt; see Figure 4), something comparable to an ancient guest worker program!
8. There was a distinction made between a foreigner in a land and a legal sojourner (*ger*) or resident alien who was taking up more permanent residence. The latter might be likened in America to the holder of a green card. In Canada, such individuals are known as "landed immigrants."
9. Foreigners who assimilated into Egyptian society and learned the Egyptian language could advance in the private sector as well as within the state bureaucracy (e.g., Aper-el and Joseph). Similarly, foreigners could come to Israel and be integrated into society (the example of Ruth the Moabite will be discussed in Chapter 5).

chapter 3

# UNWANTED GUESTS: THE STORY OF THE ISRAELITE EXODUS

"... you were aliens in Egypt." (Exod. 23:9)

When the book of Genesis ended, we found that the extended family of Jacob (Israel) had joined Joseph in Egypt with the permission of the unnamed Pharaoh. Thus they became resident aliens or legal immigrants (Hebrew, *ger*). The king not only offered them a rich tract of land on which to settle but also made job offers to Joseph's brothers. Here is what Pharaoh is reported to have said: "the land of Egypt is before you; settle your father and your brothers in the best part of the land. Let them live in Goshen. And if you know of any among them with special ability, put them in charge of my own livestock" (Gen. 47:6).

So things went well for the Hebrew clans for decades or even a century or more, and their population grew (Exod. 1:7). The Bible does not tell us how much time elapsed between the end of Genesis and the opening chapters of Exodus. But an ominous note is sounded as the book of Exodus begins that foreshadows the hardship and enslavement to come. It declares: "Then a new king, who did not know about Joseph, came to power in Egypt" (Exod. 1:8). The king was obviously paranoid about the Hebrews perhaps multiplying to the point where they could team up with his enemies and attack Egypt.

The historical context behind the king's phobia is not known with certainty, but a plausible scenario is that Egypt in the period of oppression as represented in Exodus 1–13 is Egypt of the New Kingdom or Eighteenth and Nineteenth Dynasties (ca. 1525–1250 B.C.).[1] During the century and a quarter before the New Kingdom began, Egypt had been ruled by the infamous Hyksos kings (ca. 1650–1525 B.C.). They were foreign rulers, which is what the Egyptian term *Hyksos* means. Their capital, the city of Avaris, is currently being investigated in the northeastern delta of Egypt at the site of Tell el-Dab'a. Excavations since the 1960s reveal that the Hyksos were themselves Semites, originally from Syria/Canaan.[2] They had invaded or possibly immigrated during a period of Egyptian political and economic weakness. In time they were able to take over and rule at least the northern two-thirds of Egypt's Nile Valley.

After more than a century of foreign domination, the rulers of Thebes in southern Egypt began a series of military campaigns that spanned the reigns of several kings and perhaps ten to twenty years. Pharaoh Ahmose finally succeeded in defeating the Hyksos and driving them out of Egypt around 1525 B.C. Thus he became the founder of the Eighteenth Dynasty and is recognized as the monarch who began the New Kingdom, the era of Egyptian imperialism. With all of northern Egypt under his rule, this king or one of his successors realized that the burgeoning Hebrews in time could end up domineering the Egyptian population as the Hyksos had previously done. If this reconstruction is the context of Exodus 1, then we can understand the Pharaoh's xenophobia about the Semitic-speaking Hebrew population living in the very region from which the Hyksos governed.

To curb the population growth, Pharaoh ordered that the Hebrews be conscripted into forced labor. They were assigned to make bricks for building projects and to do menial farm work for the state (Exod. 1:11–14). In addition to the forced labor, an

[1]For a discussion of this scenario, see James K. Hoffmeier, *Israel in Egypt* (New York: Oxford University Press, 1999), 52–76.

[2]See the works of the excavator Manfred Bietak, *Avaris and Piramesse: Archaeological Exploration in the Eastern Nile Delta* (London/Oxford: Oxford University Press, 1979) and *Avaris the Capital of the Hyksos: Recent Excavations at Tell El-Dab'a* (London: British Museum, 1996).

even more heinous crime was committed against the Hebrews. The king commanded that newborn baby boys were to be killed by the midwives who assisted the Hebrew mothers with the deliveries (Exod. 1:10–16). Beginning with this unnamed Pharaoh, a long period of enslavement and oppression began, and the Israelite sojourn turned bitter. This excruciating experience is memorialized in an early creed of Israel preserved in the book of Deuteronomy: "My father was a wandering Aramean, and he went down into Egypt with a few people and lived [*yagar*, "sojourned"] there and became a great nation, powerful and numerous. But the Egyptians mistreated us and made us suffer, putting us to hard labor" (26:5–6). Later Israelite hymnody also reflects the status of the Hebrews as aliens in Egypt: "Then Israel entered Egypt; Jacob lived as an alien in the land of Ham" (Psalm 105:23). The prophets also reminisced about Egypt's experience in Israel. Hosea stated, concerning the suffering in Egypt, "I lifted the yoke from their neck" (Hos. 11:4), while his colleague Micah declared, "I brought you up out of Egypt and redeemed you from the land of slavery" (Mic. 6:4).

The great protagonist of the exodus, Moses, was born in Egypt during this period of oppression. His story is well known from the classic Hollywood blockbuster *The Ten Commandments* (1956) or the more recent *Prince of Egypt* (1998). Both movies dramatically portray the oppression of the Israelites and how a grown-up Moses, having been reared in the royal court, attempted to stop an Egyptian taskmaster from beating a Hebrew worker. During this intervention, he killed the Egyptian. Fearing royal revenge, Moses fled Egypt (Exod. 2:11–15). He made his way across the Sinai Peninsula to the land of Midian in northern Arabia where he met Midianites who were distant relatives of the Hebrews.[3] Here's how the narrative reads:

[3]After the death of Sarah, Abraham married Keturah and had six sons, one of whom was Midian. He is the eponymous ancestor of the Midianites (Gen. 25:1–4). The Midianites later linked up with another branch of Abraham's family, the Ishmaelites, forming a tribal league between them. This close association is seen in later history when the terms are used synonymously (cf. Gen. 37:28; Judg. 8:22–24).

> When Pharaoh heard of this, he tried to kill Moses, but Moses fled from Pharaoh and went to live in Midian, where he sat down by a well. Now a priest of Midian had seven daughters, and they came to draw water and fill the troughs to water their father's flock. Some shepherds came along and drove them away, but Moses got up and came to their rescue and watered their flock. When the girls returned to Reuel their father, he asked them, "Why have you returned so early today?" They answered, "An Egyptian rescued us from the shepherds. He even drew water for us and watered the flock." "And where is he?" he asked his daughters. "Why did you leave him? Invite him to have something to eat." Moses agreed to stay with the man, who gave his daughter Zipporah to Moses in marriage. (Exod. 2:15–21)

Here we notice that Moses was thought to be an Egyptian by the Midianites, apparently based on his dress and hairstyle. Hence he was recognized as a foreigner. Reuel initially invited Moses for a meal as an expression of hospitality. Following that gracious gesture, however, he moved beyond that, offering Moses his daughter Zipporah in marriage. Clearly tied to this act is an invitation to live with him and work for him (see Exod. 3:1). Because Jethro was a person of authority and a resident of Midian, he could invite Moses to stay, thereby making him a legal resident alien. He was not a "foreigner" (*nekhar* or *zar*) but an "alien" (*ger*).

When his wife Zipporah bore a son, "Moses named him Gershom, saying, 'I have become an alien in a foreign land'" (Exod. 2:22). By naming his son "an alien" there (*ger* + *shom*), Moses was acknowledging his status as an alien. The explanation for his son's name comes up again in Exodus 18:3. In both passages he is described as an alien (*ger*) in a foreign (*nokhariah*) land.

Meanwhile, back in Egypt, the harsh treatment of the Hebrews continued, but we are informed that God was well aware of their suffering:

> The Israelites groaned in their slavery and cried out, and their cry for help because of their slavery went up to God. God heard their groaning and he remembered his covenant with Abraham,

> with Isaac and with Jacob. So God looked on the Israelites and was concerned about them. (Exod. 2:23–25)

In the midst of this crisis, the narrative continues by reporting God's call to Moses and the commission to return to Egypt to approach Pharaoh with the divine directive, "let my people go" (Exod. 5:1). The initial request was for a temporary leave to worship God (Exod. 5:1, 3), but the treatment grew worse instead.

> That same day Pharaoh gave this order to the slave drivers and foremen in charge of the people: "You are *no longer to supply the people with straw for making bricks; let them go and gather their own straw*. But require them to *make the same number of bricks as before; don't reduce the quota*. They are lazy; that is why they are crying out, 'Let us go and sacrifice to our God.' Make the work harder for the men so that they keep working and pay no attention to lies." (Exod. 5:6–9)

The portrayal of the demanding work imposed on the Hebrews in Exodus, along with targeted quotas and problems with straw, has a familiar ring in Egyptian documents from the same general period as the Hebrews were enslaved.[4] Even Egyptian workers had quotas to reach in brickmaking. Earlier than the era of Moses, papyrus records tally up the numbers of bricks made by work crews and show that more often than not they failed to reach their target, though one Egyptian officer in the thirteenth century B.C. boasted in a letter to Pharaoh that his workers "are making their quota of bricks daily."[5] Another officer was not so fortunate, however, and complained in a letter to his superiors that he was remaining at the work site where he had been assigned, but he was "unequipped, and there are neither men to make bricks nor straw in the neighborhood."[6]

The Egyptian administration indeed used forced labor to make bricks for building projects. They employed "slave drivers"

[4]For references to Egyptian sources, see Hoffmeier, *Israel in Egypt*, 113–115.
[5]From Papyrus Anastasi III, a translation of which is in ibid., 115.
[6]From Papyrus Anastasi IV, a translation of which is in ibid.

or taskmasters and "foremen" to oversee foreigners in such work projects. Evidence for this practice is found in the tomb of the fifteenth-century B.C. prime minister or vizier named Rekhmire. Among the wonderful painted scenes that adorn the walls of the tomb is one showing foreign workers carrying water, making mud, pressing it into brick forms, and carrying loads of bricks with the aid of shoulder yokes (Figure 9). Two of the foremen are shown with sticks. One sits idly by, keeping an eye on a group of workers, while the other is prodding or striking a worker who is walking along carrying a bucket full of mud.

**FIGURE 9**

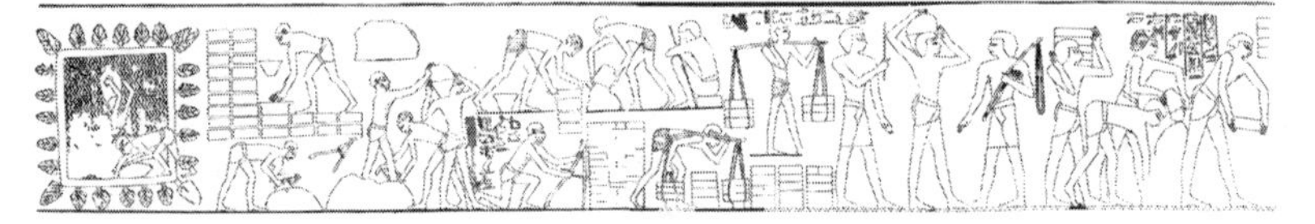

Scene from the tomb of Rekhmire in Thebes (Luxor, Egypt) showing Asiatic and Nubian forced labor crew making bricks for the construction of a temple.

Who are these workers? A close look at the representation shows that they are not portrayed as Egyptians as are the two slave drivers who wield sticks. Rather some of them are portrayed with Nubian or African racial features, while the other men are depicted as West Asians, Semitic-speaking people, likely Canaanites. Over the scene a faint inscription in hieroglyphs reports that the people depicted were taken by the king (Thutmose III, 1479–1425 B.C.) on his military campaigns. In other words, these are POWs and deportees. It appears that the Hebrews, although they had legal alien status, were subsequently treated as enemies of the state.

The Israelites were permitted to leave only after the calamitous plagues struck Egypt, over a period of possibly nine months, climaxing with the death of the eldest sons of the Egyptians (Exod. 11–12).[7] The passages quoted above from the later biblical texts demonstrate that the Israelites never forgot the marvelous deliver-

[7]Ibid., 146–149.

ance from Egypt, nor did they fail to remember that they had been aliens whose fortunes were reversed from being welcomed guests to becoming abused slaves of the Egyptian state. These two factors left an indelible impression on Israel and have a bearing on the laws that were given at Mt. Sinai.

Once out of Egypt, the Israelites found themselves in the Sinai Peninsula, a political no-man's-land that connected Africa and Asia, Egypt and Canaan. In ancient times Sinai was exploited by both the Egyptians and the Canaanites for its copper and turquoise. The mines of southern Sinai at Serabit el-Khadim and Wadi Maghara attest to the presence of valuable resources. Egyptian and Canaanite inscriptions are etched in the caves and on stones found in and around the temple of the goddess Hathor, patron of the mining region. Sinai was not under Egypt's political control as it is today. During the New Kingdom, however, Egyptian forts were situated across northern Sinai, demonstrating their control over the road between Egypt and Canaan. Their hegemony did not include the rest of Sinai. The mining area was seasonally visited by expeditions and their security forces, but this area was not occupied year-round.

Consequently no one permanently lived in Sinai in Old Testament times. It was the sphere of seasonal pastoralists—Bedouins with their flocks. On their way to Mt. Sinai, the Israelites encountered the Amalekites, one such nomadic group (Exod. 17), and a battle ensued. No doubt they fought over access to water, a scarce commodity in Sinai.

The Israelites spent forty years in the wilderness of Sinai (Num. 14:33–34; 32:13; Deut. 2:7; 8:2, 4; 29:5, Josh. 5:6), and camped for around a year at Mt. Sinai, which was probably somewhere in south central Sinai.[8] They traveled next to Kadesh Barnea, an oasis on the border between Canaan and Sinai. Here and in the immediately surrounding region they spent around thirty-eight

[8]Numbers 10:11 informs us that the Israelites departed Mt. Sinai thirteen months after they left Egypt, and Exodus 19:1 indicates that six weeks elapsed from the departure from Egypt until the arrival at Mt. Sinai. Combining these data, a period of eleven months was spent at Mt. Sinai. For a review of the evidence for the location of Mt. Sinai, see James K. Hoffmeier, *Ancient Israel in Sinai* (New York: Oxford University Press, 2005), 114–148.

years (Deut. 2:14) before marching through Jordan and entering Canaan under the leadership of Joshua.

It is highly significant that during this forty-year period in Sinai, and even though they were refugees and landless, the verb "to sojourn" (*gwr*) is never used in the Torah of the Israelites during this period, nor is the word "alien" (*ger*) ever applied to the Israelites during this period. Here is how the Torah describes the four decades in Sinai:

> They set out from Rephidim and came into the wilderness of Sinai, and *they encamped in the wilderness*. There Israel encamped before the mountain. (Exod. 19:2, ESV)
>
> And the LORD's anger was kindled against Israel, and *he made them wander in the wilderness forty years*, until all the generation that had done evil in the sight of the LORD was gone. (Num. 32:13, ESV)

These passages speak of camping and wandering in the wilderness. Even more descriptive is the following statement: "*your children shall be shepherds in the wilderness forty years*, and shall suffer for your faithlessness, until the last of your dead bodies lies in the wilderness" (Num. 14:33, ESV). Here they are viewed as pastoral nomads.

The same is true in books that follow the Torah when they reflect on Israel's wilderness experience. In the book of Judges, Jephthah observes about the Israelites that "when they came up out of Egypt, Israel went through the wilderness to the Red Sea and on to Kadesh" (11:16). In Joshua 5:6, for instance, we read, "The Israelites had moved about in the desert forty years until all the men who were of military age when they left Egypt had died, since they had not obeyed the LORD." The prophet Jeremiah around 600 B.C. condemned his contemporaries for forgetting God's past faithfulness to Israel in Sinai:

> *They did not ask, "Where is the LORD,*

*who brought us up out of Egypt*
*and led us through the barren wilderness,*
*through a land of deserts and rifts,*
*a land of drought and darkness,*
*a land where no one travels and no one lives?" (Jer. 2:6)*

In the Bible, as the foregoing passages illustrate, the Israelites did not consider themselves to be aliens when they were in Sinai because they were not living in a plainly defined land controlled by a political authority. As noted previously, a number of the narratives in Genesis show that to reside as an alien in another land one was required to receive the formal agreement of the leader or official representative of that nation. Since Sinai was not a sovereign country per se with recognized borders and a king, no authorization was required.

Clearly, the Hebrews did not view themselves as aliens during this forty-year period of their history. It is important to recognize this fact because it demonstrates that there was a legal distinction between a citizen (i.e., one who is natively born in the land of their parents), a foreigner (*nekhar* or *zar*—one traveling through the land of another or a visitor), and an alien (*ger*—one who leaves home to establish a new permanent residence with the approval of a citizen-host). As Moses and the Israelites discovered when attempting to leave Sinai and pass through Edom in the Trans-Jordan (see Chapter 2), they had left the politically neutral Sinai Peninsula and were about to enter a country with borders, and the permission of that nation's government was required even to travel through that territory (Num. 20:16–21).

## THE GIVING OF THE LAW

The main event of the wilderness experience was that God made a covenant—a legally binding agreement—with the people of Israel. In recent years biblical scholars have recognized that the structure of the material in Exodus 20ff. and Deuteronomy 5ff. follow a well-known ancient Near Eastern literary pattern used in treaty documents of the second millennium B.C.[9] In fact, the ancient Semitic term *b^e^rith*, used in ancient texts from Mesopotamia, Syria, and Egypt for "treaty," occurs in Exodus and is commonly rendered as "covenant" (e.g., 19:5; 23:32; 24:7).

The study of actual ancient treaty texts reveals a six-part structure to the documents, all of which are found in the Sinaitic Covenant or treaty beginning in Exodus 20.[10] First, the maker of the treaty is introduced by name (Exod. 20:2a: "I am the LORD [Yahweh] your God"), followed by a brief historical summary of the relationship between the parties (Exod. 20:2b: "who brought you out of Egypt, out of the land of slavery"). The third part of the pattern is a list of stipulations or laws that will govern the relationship between Israel and God. In Exodus 20:3–23:33 and Exodus 25:1–40:38; Leviticus 1–26 we see the laws that served as the foundation of Israel's social and religious life. According to most Jewish authorities, there were 613 laws from Exodus 20 through the book of Deuteronomy. If one thinks about it, this is a rather small corpus of laws to regulate an entire nation. The laws had to cover the legal institution and religious practices as well as the social and economic arenas.[11]

The biblical laws are divided between laws that are prohibitions, the "thou shalt nots," and positive declarations like "love your neighbor." Because Israel's experience as aliens in Egypt had been harsh and was indelibly impressed in their collective memory, it is not surprising that laws regarding aliens figure so prominently in the Torah. The rationale for Israel giving special consideration to aliens and their vulnerable plight in a foreign land is rooted in Israel's own experience as mistreated aliens. Although the laws regarding the alien will be treated in detail in the next chapter, here are two examples:

---

[9]Ibid., 183–192.

[10]For a complete study of the covenant formula with comparisons between ancient Near Eastern treaty texts and those found in Exodus and Deuteronomy, see Kenneth A. Kitchen, *On the Reliability of the Old Testament* (Grand Rapids, MI: Eerdmans, 2003), 283–299.

[11]The other three points of the six-part formula are: 4) depositing the treaty text and publicly reading it (25:16; 34:1, 28–29), 5) public witness to the treaty (Exod. 24:4), and 6) an oath ceremony with a list of curses and blessings (Exod. 24:1–11; Lev. 26:3–33).

> Do not mistreat an alien or oppress him, for you were aliens in Egypt. (Exod. 22:21)

> Do not oppress an alien; you yourselves know how it feels to be aliens, because you were aliens in Egypt. (Exod. 23:9)

The Israelites knew all too well from their own corporate experience as aliens in Egypt that aliens were easily victimized, and hence the laws in the Torah were given by God to protect the most vulnerable, including widows, orphans, and aliens. It was evident from the beginning of Israel's history that aliens would be a part of the community (see Chapter 4), and the many laws intended to protect aliens reflect God's concern for the resident alien. Deuteronomy 10:18 further states that God "loves the alien."

chapter 4

# LESSONS LEARNED: THE LAW AND THE ALIEN

**Do not oppress an alien; you yourselves know how it feels to be aliens, because you were aliens in Egypt. (Exod. 23:9)**

Everyone knows the celebrated teaching of Jesus in the Gospels: "love your neighbor as yourself" (Matt. 19:19; 22:39; Mark 12:31). But as readers of the Torah or the Old Testament law know, it did not originate with him in the first century A.D. Rather, the New Testament citations are actually found in Leviticus, and Jesus is quoting that passage. The entire verse reads, "Do not seek revenge or bear a grudge against one of your people, but love your neighbor as yourself. I am the LORD" (Lev. 19:18). A few paragraphs later, this remarkable law is specifically applied to aliens: "You shall love the alien as yourself, for you were aliens in the land of Egypt" (Lev. 19:34, NRSV).

## LOVE THE ALIEN

Surprisingly, biblical law has a lot to say about the alien in Israelite society. In fact, the word for alien (*ger*) occurs more than sixty times in the legal section of the Torah. Previously (Chapter 2) it was shown that an alien was a foreigner who was a legal resident of Israel. The foreigner (*nekhar* or *zar*) was not. When these terms are found in the legal section of the Pentateuch, we see that the foreigner does not enjoy the benefits and protections afforded to the alien (*ger*). For a good example that illustrates the difference in status between the foreigner and the alien, consider the laws regarding paying interest. Leviticus 25:35–37 records that Israelites should not charge interest on loans to fellow Israelites and aliens. Foreigners (*nokharim*), on the other hand, could be charged interest (Deut. 15:3). Clearly there is a difference in status between the *ger* and the *nekhar* and *zar* as reflected in the laws regarding interest. The question we need to address here is, why does the Torah offer such a sympathetic stance regarding the alien?

The oppressive treatment that the Israelites experienced as aliens in Egypt is without a doubt the main reason so many of the laws deal with the alien in Israel. After all, Israel knew what it was like to be an alien and to be harshly treated. Consequently, it is not surprising that God gave so many statutes concerning the appropriate treatment of aliens. In this chapter I will review many of the laws dealing with the alien who lived in Israel.

The two greatest commandments of the Law, according to the New Testament, are: love God and love your neighbor (Matt. 22:37–38; Luke 10:27). These two pillars of biblical law are reflected in the Ten Commandments themselves because the first four deal with the relationship between Israel and God (Exod. 20:2–11; Deut. 5:6–15), and the latter six pertain to the social arena (Exod. 20:12–17; Deut. 5:16–21). The Ten Commandments themselves might be viewed as establishing the basic categories of religious and social law. All succeeding laws are themselves logical extensions and nuances of the Ten. As one reviews all the laws about aliens, it is apparent that they can be divided into several obvious categories, which I have placed under the following rubrics: 1) general ethical considerations, 2) legal protection, 3) treatment of employees, 4) social benefits, and 5) religious participation. Having offered these different categories, it will be obvious that they often overlap, especially the religious and social spheres.[1]

[1]For a study that reviews many references to the alien in the Torah, see Georges Moucarry, "The Alien According to the Torah," *Themelios*, 14 No. 1 (1988), 17–20.

In the following sections, the term *ger* is consistently used for the alien. As was demonstrated in Chapter 2, the *ger* had legal standing in the community and therefore was afforded protection and had rights. The same is not true for the foreigner, i.e., the *nekhar* or *zar* who lacked legal status and therefore is not mentioned anywhere in the Law as having these benefits. This is a salient point in the current debate about aliens and illegal immigrants in America, especially for those who look to the Bible to establish their position on how illegal aliens should be treated by the legal system.

## GENERAL ETHICAL CONSIDERATIONS

In this group from the legal corpus, the Israelites are charged in general terms not to oppress or mistreat aliens because Israel had experienced maltreatment as aliens in Egypt. Since they had experienced injustice, intolerance, and inhumane treatment, they were expected to treat aliens differently. This is why we have such statements as:

> *Do not mistreat an alien or oppress him*, for you were aliens in Egypt. (Exod. 22:21)

> *Do not oppress an alien*; you yourselves know how it feels to be aliens, because you were aliens in Egypt. (Exod. 23:9)

A similar statement in Deuteronomy adds that the Israelites were to actually love aliens.

> And you are to *love those who are aliens*, for you yourselves were aliens in Egypt. (10:19)

A passage in Leviticus repeats what is contained in the previous passages but adds something profound:

> When an alien lives with you in your land, *do not mistreat him*. The alien living with you *must be treated as one of your native-*

> *born.* Love him as yourself, for you were aliens in Egypt. I am the LORD your God. (Lev. 19:33–34)

The word rendered "mistreat" (*tonu*) in these passages can apply to cheating or oppressing persons.[2] As Baruch Levine points out, this is especially true in economic areas and exploitation in legal matters.[3] Meanwhile, the word "oppressed" (*lakhats*) carries with it the idea of "pushing someone into a corner" and "to torment."[4] In addition to prohibiting the mistreatment and oppression of aliens and the admonition to love the sojourner, this law adds, "The alien living with you must be treated as one of your native-born." In other words, the alien must be treated as an equal to citizens; no prejudice was to be tolerated. This has been understood to mean that the prohibitions in the Law applied to the alien in Israel but not necessarily the religious proscriptions or performative laws of the Torah.[5] One reason for the inclusion of the alien in the prohibitive laws is that regardless of who the offender might be, the laws were to safeguard the holiness of God and the sanctuary, as well as the land itself. In the case of the former, consider Leviticus 20:1–3, which deals with infant sacrifice: "*Any Israelite or any alien* living in Israel who gives any of his children to Molech must be put to death . . . for by giving his children to Molech, *he has defiled my sanctuary and profaned my holy name.*"

Infant sacrifice was closely linked with the cult of the god Molech.[6] This vile practice, whether the offender was an Israelite or an alien, was a capital offense because it was murder. Furthermore, offering one's children to a pagan deity would also have a defiling effect on the sanctuary, and God's holy name or character was insulted by such behavior. So infant sacrifice was taboo in Israel.

---

[2]KB, 416.

[3]Baruch Levine, *Leviticus: The JPS Torah Commentary* (Philadelphia: Jewish Publications Society, 1989), 134.

[4]KB, 527.

[5]Jacob Milgrom, *Leviticus 1–16: The Anchor Bible Commentary* (New York: Doubleday, 1991), 1055.

[6]For a thorough study of the cult of Molech, see George C. Heider, *The Cult of Molek: A Reassessment*, Supp. 43 (Sheffield: JSOT, 1985).

The purity of the land is in mind in Leviticus 18:26–27, which stresses the importance of not engaging in deplorable practices such as infant sacrifice and of obeying the God-given laws:

> But you must keep my decrees and my laws. *The native-born and the aliens living among you must not do any of these detestable things*, for all these things were done by the people who lived in the land before you, and *the land became defiled*.

Thus the legal corpus provides the social and religious grounds for the alien participating in the same legal code of conduct, but these do not offer a theological or moral basis for not mistreating but rather loving the alien. True, the Hebrews when aliens had been victims themselves, which explains the commands against oppressing the alien, but it does not explain why the alien should be loved. It might be suggested that the foundation for the treatment of the alien is rooted in the biblical anthropology established in Genesis 1:27: "So God created man in his own image, in the image of God he created him; male and female he created them." While theologians and commentators have for centuries wrestled with the meaning of "image of God," there is little doubt that it implies that all humans, regardless of race or gender, share certain attributes of the Creator or in some way represent him on earth.[7]

It has been recently recognized that because the word "image" (*tselem*) is associated with statues of kings and deities in the ancient Near East, "each person bears the stamp of royalty."[8] As such, humans have a special status in God's creation and have responsibility over creation—they are stewards of it. It logically follows, then, that because of the elevated position humans occupy, each human life has value, and that is why taking the life of another was prohibited:

> And from each man, too, I will demand an accounting for the life of his fellow man.

[7]*NIDOTTE*, I, 969.

[8]Nahum Sarna, *Genesis: The JPS Torah Commentary* (Philadelphia: Jewish Publications Society, 1989), 12.

*Whoever sheds the blood of man,*
*by man shall his blood be shed;*
*for in the image of God*
*has God made man. (Gen. 9:6–7)*

The egalitarian ideal of Leviticus 19:33 was not only to permeate the thinking of Israelites at the personal and relational levels, it also laid the foundation for the legal arena.

## LEGAL MATTERS

Because of the unique biblical understanding of the equality of all humans, even immigrants who resided in Israel with legal standing were to be treated with respect and were to be loved. In God the Creator's eyes there was parity among peoples, and this value carried over into the legal arena. This divine perspective is captured in the following law:

> The community is to have the *same rules for you and for the alien living among you*; this is a lasting ordinance for the generations to come. *You and the alien shall be the same before the* *Lord*. . . . (Num. 15:15–16)

The laws of Israel were to be applied equally to Israelite and alien alike. The implied reason is that they are considered "the same before the Lord." God does not show partiality among peoples. This is surprising when we recognize that God had a unique covenant relationship with Israel. The point is that should the foreigner attain alien status, he or she would receive the benefits and obligations of an Israelite. The same is true when a crime is unintentionally committed and lesser penalties are imposed: "One and the same law applies to everyone who sins *unintentionally*, whether he is *a native-born Israelite or an alien*" (Num. 15:29).

Of primary significance is the fact that there was to be what we in America call "equal justice under the law," which is the motto engraved over the entrance to the Supreme Court in Washington,

D.C. This foundational principle occurs in several different books of the Torah.

> *The same law applies to the native-born and to the alien* living among you. (Exod. 12:49)
>
> But you must keep my decrees and my laws. *The native-born and the aliens living among you must not do any of these detestable things*. (Lev. 18:26)
>
> You are to have *the same law for the alien and the native-born*. I am the LORD your God. (Lev. 24:22)

The principle of equal justice was not universally practiced in the ancient Near East. In the Code of Hammurabi and other Mesopotamian legal traditions, for example, people are classified as priests, citizens, two lower-class groups (*mushkenum* and *khupshu*), and slaves. Penalties for the same crime differed depending on one's social or class status. Furthermore, aliens are not even mentioned as a legally protected group of individuals in the law codes.

In biblical law aliens were to have all the legal protections of native-born Israelites; on the other hand, aliens were subject to the same regulations, and if they were guilty of an offense, the same justice was meted out against them. This is what is meant by "the same law applies to the native-born and the alien" in Exodus 12:49[9] and the above cited Leviticus passages. Likewise the alien is included in the command, "keep my decrees and my laws" (Lev. 18:26). The distinction between "decrees" *(khuqot)* and commands (*mitsvot*) is thought to be that the former refers to case law (i.e., decrees), while the latter are the prohibitions (i.e., commands). This means that while the alien was to be treated in an equal manner legally, the expectation was for the foreign resident to adhere to all the rules and regulations of Israelite law. Simply put, they were to receive equal protection under the law, but they

[9]In this context, Passover observance, and hence religious law, is in view.

were also equally responsible to respect and uphold the laws in totality. Aliens could not, for instance, ignore certain social laws because they differed from those of their native culture or because they disagreed with an aspect of Israelite law. They could not pick and choose which laws to obey and yet remain in good standing with the covenant community.

Above Leviticus 24:22 was quoted, which states that there should be "the same law for the alien and the native-born." This qualifier actually serves as a reminder of the equal treatment provision at the end of the establishment of a legal precedent. Beginning in verse 10, the narrative recounts the case of a man who violated the Law. The offender was the son of an Israelite woman, but his father was an Egyptian. Because of the complexity of the case, it was not clear how this man should be treated. Was he an Egyptian, an Israelite, an alien, or a foreigner? He was placed in custody, and the matter was brought to Moses, who might be regarded as the chief justice at that time (cf. Exod. 18:20–26).[10] Moses, as was his practice, brought the unprecedented legal problem to God for clarification. The decision handed down was that the biracial man fit into the category of native-born/alien, and so the principle of "same law" was deemed applicable (it had been previously enshrined in the Law, Exod. 12:19; Lev. 18:26).

This interesting case illustrates how a complex legal matter that involved a person who did not neatly fit into the normal categories was resolved. It further shows that this case was dealt with thoughtfully and with appeals to the highest legal authority.

*Justice for All*

In the Law and, as we shall see later, in the prophets, justice for the alien was also linked with the fatherless and widows. God expects just treatment for everyone *vis-à-vis* the Law by people in general and by the courts because he himself shows no partiality among people:

[10]In this passage we learn that Moses appointed wise and able men to arbitrate and settle cases, but the complicated juridical matters were brought to him for resolution.

> For the LORD your God is God of gods and Lord of lords, the great God, mighty and awesome, *who shows no partiality and accepts no bribes. He defends the cause of the fatherless and the widow, and loves the alien*, giving him food and clothing. (Deut. 10:17–18)

Because God "shows no partiality and accepts no bribes," he expects the same of the people of Israel as well as of the judges. The specific reference to the fatherless, widow, and alien is because these individuals were the most vulnerable within a society. The widow and fatherless lacked a husband or father to represent their interests and to protect them. So God becomes their defender. It is also evident that God provides for the basic needs of these vulnerable victims of society, making sure that they are clothed and fed. Below we shall see that the Israelites were to help provide for these needs (see *Social Concerns*), and that judges should show fairness.

Toward the end of his life Moses reflected back to the beginning of the wilderness period when he set up the judicial system (cf. Exod. 18):

> So I took the leading men of your tribes, wise and respected men, and appointed them to have authority over you—as commanders of thousands, of hundreds, of fifties and of tens and as tribal officials. And I charged your judges at that time: Hear the disputes between your brothers and *judge fairly*, whether the case is between brother Israelites or between one of them and an alien. *Do not show partiality in judging*; hear both small and great alike. Do not be afraid of any man, for judgment belongs to God. (Deut. 1:15–17)

According to this instruction, judges must have integrity and show no partiality to people. Those who arbitrate cases have tremendous power and can affect lives profoundly.

Later in Deuteronomy, a curse is actually pronounced on the one "who withholds justice from the alien, the fatherless or the widow" (Deut. 27:19). This curse occurs among a group of eleven specific crimes that are of a clandestine nature and hence can easily be covered up.[11] Bribery and judicial and governmental partiality are not easily detected as they are typically done secretively. What is intriguing about this curse is that it is not specifically directed at judges, but it surely includes them. This statement is directed at the entire community, for anyone can pervert justice by giving false testimony, making false charges, twisting the truth, and in scores of other ways that would deprive the defenseless. The inclusion of aliens demonstrates that God intended that they not be exploited in the legal system of ancient Israel.

### *The Practice of Sanctuary*

In 1996 Congress passed the Illegal Immigration Reform and Immigrant Responsibility Act, which requires local governments to cooperate with federal officials in apprehending illegal immigrants. This law notwithstanding, scores of cities large and small across the nation in defiance of federal law have declared their municipalities to be "sanctuary" cities for illegal aliens. This means that local officials will not cooperate with federal agents who seek to apprehend undocumented individuals, thus providing a place of sanctuary or legal protection for them. Similarly, some churches have offered their facilities to illegal aliens to avoid their arrest and deportation. Churches providing sanctuary to individuals trying to evade the law, especially where corrupt legal systems are involved, claim a long tradition within Christendom. I suspect that advocates of the sanctuary movement today do not realize that the practice originates in ancient Israelite law, and they are probably unaware that that the practice of sanctuary in the Old Testament had specific requirements and was not open to anyone regardless of their crime.

The idea and practice of sanctuary is rooted in the Law given at Mt. Sinai. Exodus 21:12–14 records the following:

> Anyone who strikes a man and kills him shall surely be put to death. However, if he *does not do it intentionally*, but God lets

[11] Jeffrey Tigay, *Deuteronomy: The JPS Torah Commentary* (Philadelphia: Jewish Publications Society, 1996), 253.

> it happen, *he is to flee to a place I will designate. But if a man schemes and kills another man deliberately, take him away from my altar* and put him to death.

This passage, along with others in ancient Israelite law, shows that murder was a capital offense; hence one of the Ten Commandments is, "You shall not murder" (Exod. 20:13). The Bible does, however, distinguish between premeditated murder and accidental death or manslaughter (in addition to Exod. 21:12–14, cf. Num. 35:15–16, 20–21, 30) and negligent homicide (e.g., Exod. 21:33–36). Only intentional or premeditated killing was punishable by death. Exodus 21:12–14 contains the first reference to the statute of sanctuary. From it we also learn that one who accidentally kills another person can flee to the sanctuary and approach the altar—originally this was the Tabernacle, Israel's tent-shrine, and then later the Temple in Jerusalem. This provision also specified that once out of Sinai and into the Promised Land, additional places of legal refuge would be designated. Put another way, the sanctuary would be extended to other locations to facilitate access to them. When those cities are identified on the eve of the entry into Canaan, Moses offers a further explanation about the practice of sanctuary.

> [S]elect some towns to be your cities of refuge, to which a person *who has killed someone accidentally* may flee. *They will be places of refuge from the avenger, so that a person accused of murder may not die before he stands trial before the assembly.* These six towns you give *will be your cities of refuge.* Give three on this side of the Jordan and three in Canaan as cities of refuge. These six towns will be a place of refuge *for Israelites, aliens and any other people living among them,* so that *anyone who has killed another accidentally* can flee there. (Num. 35:11–15)

The following two paragraphs (vv. 22–29) offer an extensive description of the conditions for receiving sanctuary.

> *But if without hostility someone suddenly shoves another or throws something at him unintentionally or, without seeing*

> *him, drops a stone on him that could kill him, and he dies, then since he was not his enemy and he did not intend to harm him,* the assembly must judge between him and the avenger of blood according to these regulations. *The assembly must protect the one accused of murder from the avenger of blood and send him back to the city of refuge to which he fled.* He must stay there until the death of the high priest, who was anointed with the holy oil.
>
> But if the accused ever goes outside the limits of the city of refuge to which he has fled and the avenger of blood finds him outside the city, the avenger of blood may kill the accused without being guilty of murder. The accused must stay in his city of refuge until the death of the high priest; only after the death of the high priest may he return to his own property. These are to be legal requirements for you throughout the generations to come, wherever you live.

Some years after moving into Canaan, the cities of refuge are designated by Joshua, the successor of Moses. After the cities are named, Joshua reiterates the purpose of these cities of legal protections:

> Then the LORD said to Joshua: "Tell the Israelites to designate the cities of refuge, as I instructed you through Moses, so that *anyone who kills a person accidentally and unintentionally may flee there and find protection from the avenger of blood.*
>
> When he flees to one of these cities, he is to stand in the entrance of the city gate and *state his case before the elders of that city.* Then they are to admit him into their city and give him a place to live with them. If the avenger of blood pursues him, they must not surrender the one accused, because he killed his neighbor unintentionally and without malice aforethought. He is to stay in that city until he has stood trial before the assembly and until the death of the high priest who is serving at that time. Then he may go back to his own home in the town from which he fled. . . . .
>
> *Any of the Israelites or any alien living among them who killed someone accidentally* could flee to these designated cities and *not be killed by the avenger of blood prior to standing trial before the assembly.* (Josh. 20:1–6, 9)

Ancient Israel, like most ancient societies, practiced some version of *lex talionis*, the law of retaliation, or the "eye for an eye" principle. In some cultures, the practice was to extract more than a pound of flesh for a pound of flesh. Put another way, the punishment exceeded the crime. When the Mosaic Law introduced the law of retaliation, it was intended to limit punishment to fit the crime. Hence Exodus 21:23–25 provides a lengthy list that covers nearly every possible bodily injury:

> . . . if there is serious injury, you are to take life for life, eye for eye, tooth for tooth, hand for hand, foot for foot, burn for burn, wound for wound, bruise for bruise.

In tribal societies, as is the case in parts of the Middle East and Asia to this day, a family member was obliged to avenge the crime against a family member. In the passages quoted here from Exodus, Numbers, and Joshua, this person is called "the avenger." The purpose of the practice of sanctuary at the Temple or the cities of refuge scattered throughout the country was to provide places where the person who had *accidentally* killed someone could flee and be protected from a retaliation that was unwarranted. A contemporary analogy for this practice is when a defendant seeks a change of venue to facilitate a fair trial. Although the person was perhaps guilty of killing, he had not murdered according to biblical law. To ensure a fair trial and to make sure the avenger of the deceased would not exercise *lex talionis*, a defendant was to flee ahead of the avenger to one of the sanctuary locations and "state his case before the elders of that city" (Josh. 20:4). Plainly the purpose of sanctuary was for the defendant to have his case heard by an impartial body of elders.

The biblical practice of sanctuary, then, was to protect the offender from vigilante justice and to ensure that he received a fair trial. Should a person come to the sanctuary who was guilty of intentionally murdering someone, he would be removed from the protection of the sanctuary and receive his punishment. This practice is clearly spelled out in Exodus 21:14: "take him away from my altar and put him to death."

One such case is that of Joab, King David's general. Joab had innocent blood on his hands (1 Kings 2:5), but David had never held him accountable. Just before the great king died, he asked his son Solomon to deal with Joab (1 Kings 2:6). When Solomon ordered that Joab be apprehended, Joab fled to the Tabernacle in Jerusalem for sanctuary. He approached the altar and took hold of its corners or horns (1 Kings 2:28). Solomon's general Benaiah was ordered to remove him from the sanctuary and kill him because "of the guilt of the innocent blood that Joab shed" (1 Kings 2:31). This narrative illustrates that sanctuary was practiced according to the provisions of the Law.

From the foregoing review of the biblical laws and passages that deal with the practice of sanctuary in ancient Israel, it is clear that its purpose was limited to offenders who had accidentally or unintentionally killed someone, thereby providing a place where their case can be heard. Sanctuary was never intended as a place to avoid the law but to allow the law to takes its proper course rather than retaliation when it was not called for. While both Israelite citizens and aliens qualified for sanctuary (cf. Num. 35:15 and Josh. 20:9), being an illegal alien was not a criterion for such protection. Consequently, American cities and churches who offer sanctuary for illegal immigrants cannot claim to be following the practice described in the Bible. Rather they are twisting biblical statutes and subverting federal law.

## FAIR TREATMENT OF EMPLOYEES

The main attraction for immigrants coming to America for over two centuries surely has been for economic opportunity, employment. The same is true in recent decades in Canada and Western Europe. In the U.S. many in the business world have quietly welcomed illegal immigrants because they know they can pay them the minimum wage, or less in some cases, thereby increasing their profits. Citizens would demand and receive higher pay from an employer.

I have personally seen this kind of exploitation. In high school my son was looking around for summer employment. A retailer offered him a position on the condition that he would receive payment in cash under the table and at an hourly rate less than the minimum wage. No benefits would be covered, including payment of Social Security. This kind of exploitation is both unethical and illegal but sadly is widespread today.

The motivation behind employers abusing their workers in this manner is their preoccupation with the bottom line, their profit margin. Depriving or withholding wages of hired workers is addressed in biblical law and is a theme carried over into the New Testament. Leviticus 19:13 equates depriving a hired man of his pay with robbery: "Do not defraud your neighbor or rob him. Do not hold back the wages of a hired man overnight." During much of the period covered in Old Testament history (ca. 1200–400 B.C.), most people worked on their own family farm or as artisans of some sort. During the harvest season, a large landowner might hire day laborers to assist with the fieldwork, or a person who could afford it might hire workers for a building project. Such workers would have been paid at the end of each day for the work done. Not until after the sixth and fifth centuries B.C. was coinage introduced in Judah and used as a means of payment. Prior to that, wages were reckoned in commodities that could be used, consumed, or bartered. In whatever form the payment came, it would have been paid daily.

The practice of receiving one's wages at the end of a workday is depicted in the Parable of the Workers told by Jesus in the Gospel of Matthew. It starts out by describing a landowner hiring workers for the day: "For the kingdom of heaven is like a landowner who went out early in the morning to hire men to work in his vineyard. He agreed to pay them a denarius for the day and sent them into his vineyard" (20:1–2). Over the course of the day, the landowner hired additional workers until the workday ended around 6:00 P.M. Then we read, "When evening came, the owner of the vineyard said to his foreman, 'Call the workers and pay them their wages, beginning with the last ones hired and going on to the first'" (v. 8). Each received the day's wage of a denarius, a silver coin,[12] that evening.

The system of daily paying workers a standard (minimum) wage is reflected in the Mosaic Law in the passage quoted above: "Do not hold back the wages of a hired man overnight" (Lev. 19:13b). Nowhere in the Law does it specify what the standard amount should be for a day's work, only that payment should be made daily.

The law of Leviticus is expanded in Deuteronomy, which reads:

> Do not take advantage of a hired man who is poor and needy, whether he is a brother Israelite or *an alien living in one of your towns*. Pay him his wages each day before sunset, because he is poor and is counting on it. Otherwise *he may cry to the* LORD against you, and you will be guilty of sin. (Deut. 24:14–15)

Here the Law specifies that day workers should be paid before sunset, and the alien is included here. Like other poor and needy workers who are not employed year-round, the alien desperately needed his pay; he "urgently depends on it" (JPSV) and, as Peter Craigie noted, needs immediate payment "each day to feed a family each day."[13] The employer who does not pay his workers daily, this law declares, "will be guilty of sin." The sense is that one would be guilty of sin that would lead to divine retribution.[14] The cry of the poor goes up to God, begging for justice to be done.

## SOCIAL BENEFITS

Ancient Israel had a unique social welfare or social security system, a safety net to assist the poorest in society whose income was insufficient to provide the essentials for living. Because Israel in the Old

---

[12]Here is not the place to discuss why in Jesus' parable the people who worked just one hour were paid the same as those who had worked all day, presumably twelve hours. My point in citing this parable is that it illustrates the idea of daily payment of a standard ware for labor.
[13]Peter Craigie, *The Book of Deuteronomy* (Grand Rapids, MI: Eerdmans, 1976), 309.
[14]Tigay, *Deuteronomy*, 147.

Testament period had an agricultural-based economy, the Torah provided a way for those in poverty to have access to much needed food. The first approach was reserving some of the produce of fields and trees for the needy. The practice of gleaning is described in several passages.

> When you reap the harvest of your land, do not reap to the very edges of your field or gather the gleanings of your harvest. Do not go over your vineyard a second time or pick up the grapes that have fallen. *Leave them for the poor and the alien*. I am the LORD your God. (Lev. 19:9–10)

> When you reap the harvest of your land, do not reap to the very edges of your field or gather the gleanings of your harvest. Leave them for the poor and the alien. I am the LORD your God. (Lev. 23:22)

> When you are harvesting in your field and you overlook a sheaf, do not go back to get it. *Leave it for the alien, the fatherless and the widow*, so that the LORD your God may bless you in all the work of your hands. When you beat the olives from your trees, do not go over the branches a second time. Leave what remains for *the alien, the fatherless and the widow*. When you harvest the grapes in your vineyard, do not go over the vines again. *Leave what remains for the alien, the fatherless and the widow. Remember that you were slaves in Egypt*. That is why I command you to do this. (Deut. 24:19–22)

The Leviticus passages single out the poor and the alien as the recipient of such aid, while Deuteronomy specifies the alien, the fatherless, and the widow, i.e., those who normally were not landowners. It is noteworthy that with this statute the landowners did not harvest the entirety of their fields or groves and give a certain percentage to the local authorities or religious officials to redistribute. Rather those who qualified for this assistance actually had to go out into the fields or climb trees and work for their food. And gleaning was hard work to judge from the way it is described in the book of Ruth (2:7, 17), which is the subject of the following chapter. The law does not specify how much should be left for the needy to harvest, but the rabbinic tradition was that one-sixtieth of the field was the minimum.[15]

These texts describe a humanitarian practice that was known elsewhere in the biblical world in ancient times. A Sumerian "Farmer's Almanac," for example, encourages the farmer to allow gleaners into the fields, even permitting them to sleep there at night during harvest, much like what is found in the story of Ruth (3:1–13). Divine blessing was offered to the Sumerians who allowed the poor into their fields to glean.[16] What makes the Israelite practice unique is the inclusion of the alien in gleaning from the harvests, and for the Hebrews it is clear from the location of the gleaning laws in Leviticus 19 that it was considered to be a religious and ethical duty.[17]

A second area where the disadvantaged could receive assistance was from the tithe or tenth that every family was expected to contribute from the produce of their fields. This was to occur every three years, as Deuteronomy 26:12–13 commands:

> When you have finished setting aside a tenth of all your produce in the third year, the year of the tithe, *you shall give it to the Levite, the alien, the fatherless and the widow, so that they may eat in your towns* and be satisfied. Then say to the LORD your God: "I have removed from my house the sacred portion and have given it to the Levite, the alien, the fatherless and the widow, according to all you commanded. I have not turned aside from your commands nor have I forgotten any of them."

The tithe described here occurred every three years and was handled on a local basis. That is, the cereals and fruits were not taken to a central sanctuary for redistribution to the disadvantaged. This tithe was shared, as the text specifies, "so that they may eat in your towns and be satisfied." In other words, it was handled locally, not nationally.

---

[15]Jacob Milgrom, *Leviticus 17–22*, *The Anchor Bible Commentary* (New York: Doubleday, 2001), 1626.

[16]For a translation, see S. N. Kramer, *The Sumerians* (Chicago: University of Chicago Press, 1963), 340–342. This particular section is at the bottom of 341.

[17]Milgrom, *Leviticus 17–22*, 1624.

Once again we see the usual three categories of recipients of assistance, including the alien, with the addition "the Levite." Levites were the clergy who worked at the sanctuary. The tithes were how Israel's clergy drew their salaries. Another reason for the inclusion of the Levites is that they, like the alien, the fatherless, and the widow, did not receive a tribal territory (Josh. 13:14) and thus did not own fields and property except for their homes.

The poor, including aliens, were sustained in ancient Israel by the practice of gleaning and the tithe. If we are looking for a principle to apply in the American context regarding the treatment of aliens, there clearly is a basis for legal immigrants who are needy receiving the same social benefits that the government offers to disadvantaged citizens. "Foreigners," on the other hand, are not mentioned as beneficiaries of this social generosity.

## RELIGIOUS INCLUSION

From the foregoing discussions, it is clear that the alien was to receive certain legal protections and social benefits. But it does not stop there. References in the Torah demonstrate that aliens could be integrated into the religious life of Israel.

Surely the most important religious observance in the Jewish faith was and remains Passover, the annual observance of the exodus from Egypt. When Passover was instituted in the book of Exodus, we learn that aliens could participate in this most enduring ritual:

> *An alien living among you who wants to celebrate the* LORD's Passover must have all the males in his household circumcised; then he may take part like one born in the land. No uncircumcised male may eat of it. (Exod.12:48)

It is evident from this passage that once a male alien was circumcised, he was fully included in the religious life of ancient Israel. Circumcision was introduced as a sign of the covenant between God and Abraham and his descendants in Genesis 17:

> This is my covenant with you and your descendants after you, the covenant you are to keep: Every male among you shall be circumcised. *You are to undergo circumcision, and it will be the sign of the covenant between me and you.* For the generations to come every male among you who is eight days old must be circumcised, including those born in your household or bought with money from a foreigner—those who are not your offspring. *Whether born in your household or bought with your money, they must be circumcised.* My covenant in your flesh is to be an everlasting covenant. (vv. 10–13)

Here circumcision applied to all Abraham's household and any servants, including the foreigners among them. This same inclusive spirit apparently stands behind the exodus passage that provided for the inclusion of aliens. Consequently, when the alien through circumcision demonstrated that he worshiped the God with whom the covenant had been made, "then he may take part [in the Passover] like one born in the land" (Exod. 12:13).

When a *ger* was circumcised, the Greek (Septuagint) translates the Hebrew *ger* as "proselyte" in the Law when the context is religious, whereas *xenos* or *paroikos* is used in other settings.[18] This translation reflects the later equation of *ger* or *alien* with a convert to Judaism, a proselyte.

The religious inclusion was not unconditional in the Law. If the alien violated the religious laws of Passover, the following prescription is given:

> For seven days no yeast is to be found in your houses. And whoever eats anything with yeast in it *must be cut off from the community of Israel, whether he is an alien or native-born.* (Exod. 12:19)

The expression "be cut off" derives from a somewhat obscure form of the word "cut" (*karat*) that suggests the individual would be excluded from religious observances,[19] something akin to

[18]"Proselyte," in *Anchor Bible Dictionary*, 5, ed. D. N. Freedman (New York: Doubleday, 1992), 503.
[19]KB, 501.

excommunication in the Christian tradition. In the rabbinic tradition, however, this punishment is interpreted to be a more severe form of divine judgment of some sort.[20] Regardless of the precise meaning, it is apparent that aliens could be included in the celebration of Passover if the men were circumcised, thereby accepting the God of Israel and entering into the covenant community; but if they violated the ceremonial rules, they would certainly be barred from future participation. The same is true of the native-born.

The important point is, however, that the alien was welcome to join Passover observances provided one followed the prescriptions of the Law. The foreigner (*nekhar*), on the other hand, was not permitted to participate in Passover at all. Exodus 12:43 excludes him: "The LORD said to Moses and Aaron, 'These are the regulations for the Passover: No foreigner is to eat of it.'"

The incorporation of the alien into the religious life of Israel did not end with Passover. Without a doubt the Day of Atonement or *yom kippur* was the most solemn of religious observances. This was the one day a year that the High Priest entered the Holy of Holies of the sanctuary to bring the blood of a sacrificed bull and to sprinkle some on the lid of the Ark of the Covenant to make atonement for the whole nation (Lev. 16:15–16, 34). At the end of the priestly instructions the following provision is included:

> This is to be a lasting ordinance for you: On the tenth day of the seventh month you must deny yourselves and not do any work—*whether native-born or an alien living among you*—because on this day atonement will be made for you, to cleanse you. Then, before the LORD, you will be clean from all your sins. (Lev. 16:29–30)

### *Offerings and Sacrifices*

In addition to participation in the major religious rituals, the resident aliens, like other Israelites, were encouraged to present various types of offerings to God, according to Leviticus 22:17–19:

[20]Sarna, *Exodus*, 58.

> The LORD said to Moses, "Speak to Aaron and his sons and to all the Israelites and say to them: 'If any of you—*either an Israelite or an alien living in Israel—presents a gift for a burnt offering to the LORD*, either to fulfill a vow or as a freewill offering, you must present a male without defect from the cattle, sheep or goats in order that it may be accepted on your behalf.'"

The significance of this provision goes beyond the obvious inclusion of the alien in Israel's religious practices. The freewill offering (*nedevah*) was actually a "voluntary contribution to the sanctuary."[21] Thus the alien, like native-born Israelites, was not just offering gifts to God out of gratitude, but at the same time he was contributing to the operation of the sanctuary itself. The implication is clear. Even though aliens were typically thought of as poor and as candidates for the social provisions outlined in the Torah (as discussed above), they were at the same time encouraged to give back to the Temple. The working principle here is that those who benefit from the social and religious institutions of Israel should also give back as an act of appreciation.

In this section we have seen how an initiated alien could be integrated into the religious life of Israel and a number of examples of how aliens could participate in the most important observances, Passover and the Day of Atonement, which suggests that they could also share in all the Torah-ordained religious activities of the community.

### *Dietary Restrictions*

The other side of participation, that is, exclusion, is also documented in the Law. While this provision was briefly discussed in the previous section, this theme is developed in great detail in Leviticus 17:8–16. Instead of citing this passage as a whole, each unit will be treated with a brief commentary. Notice that these laws are all addressed to the Israelite and to the alien living among them.

---

[21]Levine, *Leviticus*, 44.

> Say to them: "*Any Israelite or any alien living among them* who offers a burnt offering or sacrifice and *does not bring it to the entrance to the Tent of Meeting to sacrifice it to the* LORD—that man must be cut off from his people." (17:8–9)

This law requires that burnt offerings and sacrifices be brought to the Tent of Meeting, an alternative expression for the Tabernacle. After the construction of the Temple in Solomon's day (ca. 960 B.C.), the worshipper would have brought the animals for sacrifice to the Temple court. This Levitical law meant that worshippers, aliens included, could not present their offerings to God at the location of their choosing but only at the sanctuary.

> *Any Israelite or any alien living among them who eats any blood*—I will set my face against that person who eats blood and will cut him off from his people. For the life of a creature is in the blood, and I have given it to you to make atonement for yourselves on the altar; it is the blood that makes atonement for one's life. Therefore I say to the Israelites, "*None of you may eat blood, nor may an alien living among you eat blood.*" (17:10–12)

The dietary prohibitions of the Law, a ban not attested among Israel's neighbors,[22] also applied to the alien. Among them was not consuming the blood of an animal. Here the rationale for this ban is that "the life of a creature is in the blood." Since all life belongs to God, the blood of animals must not be ingested. It is widely recognized that this ban is tied to God's covenant with Noah in the book of Genesis, where the consumption of animal blood is outlawed for all humanity (9:3–6).

The same restriction is placed on animals that are killed by hunting in the next law, and the same explanation is offered:

> *Any Israelite or any alien living among you who hunts any animal or bird that may be eaten must drain out the blood and cover it with earth*, because the life of every creature is its blood.

[22]Milgrom, *Leviticus 1–16*, 706.

> That is why I have said to the Israelites, "You must not eat the blood of any creature, because the life of every creature is its blood; anyone who eats it must be cut off." (17:13–14)

In both of these commands, the alien was obligated on religious grounds to observe these dietary considerations, just like all Israelites. Another dietary restriction on the alien was not to eat the flesh of animals that had been slain by wild animals (17:15–16).

### *Sabbath Observance*

Enshrined in the Ten Commandments is the law regarding the Sabbath:

> Remember the Sabbath day by keeping it holy. Six days you shall labor and do all your work, but the seventh day is a Sabbath to the LORD your God. On it you shall not do any work, neither you, nor your son or daughter, nor your manservant or maidservant, nor your animals, *nor the alien within your gates*. For in six days the LORD made the heavens and the earth, the sea, and all that is in them, but he rested on the seventh day. Therefore the LORD blessed the Sabbath day and made it holy. (Exod. 20:8–11)

The Sabbath was not original with the Law, as verse 11 reminds us. Instead it goes back to creation. In the Genesis creation narratives God is reported as creating the earth in six days and then resting on the seventh:

> Thus the heavens and the earth were completed in all their vast array. By the seventh day God had finished the work he had been doing; so on the seventh day he rested from all his work. And God blessed the seventh day and made it holy, because on it he rested from all the work of creating that he had done. (Gen. 2:1–3)

The idea is that in creation God set an example for humans to work for six days, followed by a day of rest. Apparently whatever memory the Israelites had of the creation-Sabbath observance was lost in Egypt because when they departed, the Sabbath was reintroduced in Exodus 16 prior to the giving of the Law in Exodus 20. The reality is that the Fourth Commandment is a reinforcement of a principle established at creation.

Under the influence of this central tenet of the creation story and the Sinai law code, western civilizations to some degree have practiced Sabbath observance. Thus Jews observed and continue to observe Saturday as the seventh day. The Sabbath principle in Christianity was shifted to Sunday because Jesus rose from the dead on the first day of the week, i.e., Sunday (Matt. 28:1–7; Mark 16:2–7, 9; Luke 24:1–7; John 20:1–2; cf. Acts 20:7). Blue laws of the nineteenth and twentieth centuries in the United States and Canada were intended to limit business and other work so that individuals and families could rest and thereby observe the Fourth Commandment. This decree continues by also barring the alien from work on the Sabbath:

> On it you shall not do any work, neither you, nor your son or daughter, nor your manservant or maidservant, nor your animals, *nor the alien within your gates*. (Exod. 20:10b)

This clause of the commandment illustrates that the benefits of Sabbath rest were to be extended to the entire community, including servants and aliens.[23] The inclusion of servants and aliens shows that all humans were God's creation and were to enjoy the blessing of the Sabbath. An egalitarian view of all humanity is further suggested by the inclusion of aliens and servants in the Fourth Commandment. Exodus 23:12 adds an additional purpose for the Sabbath, namely, rest that results in refreshment or revitalization of the individual:

> Six days do your work, but on the seventh day do not work, so that your ox and your donkey *may rest and the slave born in your household, and the alien as well, may be refreshed.*

[23]This provision is also found in the parallel passage in Deuteronomy 5:14.

The inclusion of these members of the community demonstrates that God wants everyone to benefit from Sabbath rest, not just the Israelites.

## CONCLUSIONS

In this chapter we have seen that Israel received the moral mandate to love aliens who lived in Israel and not to oppress them. This principle is extended in the legal sphere where there was to be equal treatment under the Law. No legal bias toward the alien was acceptable. I would argue that we in the West, therefore, should demand no less of our legal system.

Biblical law made provisions for the alien to receive the same social benefits, such as gleaning rights, that were offered to other needy people in Israel. This humanitarian element suggests that our state and federal governments should treat the legal alien in the same manner as it does citizens. This would include such benefits as Social Security, medical aid, tuition breaks in state universities, and the like.

In the last section on religion we saw that aliens were encouraged to be fully incorporated into the religious life of Israel. They could also participate in offerings and sacrifices, celebrating Passover and observing the Day of Atonement and Sabbath, but the religious restrictions imposed on the Israelites also applied to the alien as well. From these laws we can determine two important lessons. The first is theological—namely, God views aliens in the same manner as his covenant people, Israel, and accepts their worship. Second, people could be part of the faith community based on faith in the God of Israel and obedience to the Torah and not on ethnicity.

These principles have obvious implications for the faith community today. If God receives all people based upon faith regardless of ethnicity, religious organizations should likewise welcome aliens and assist in their transition to their new land.

chapter 5

# ALIENS IN ANCIENT ISRAEL

**Aliens will join them and unite with the house of Jacob. (Isa. 14:1b)**

The Law provided for the incorporation of the alien into the community of Israel so they could benefit legally, socially, and religiously (see Chapter 4). These indeed are highly ethical, if not lofty, laws showing compassion and promoting inclusion. But is there any evidence that aliens were in fact included in Israelite society and treated in a manner consistent with the ideals espoused in the Law? The answer is yes, for the most part. In what follows we shall review some of the evidence, and it started in Egypt at the very beginning of Israel's history as a nation, which is why the Passover laws given in Egypt prior to the exodus included conditions for aliens (Exod. 12:48).

## ALIENS IN ISRAEL'S EARLY HISTORY

When the tribes of Israel departed Egypt at the exodus, we are informed that "many *other people* went up with them, as well as large droves of livestock, both flocks and herds" (Exod. 12:38). An alternative translation of the word *'erav* is "mixed multitude" (RSV, KJV, ESV). Mention of these non-Israelites suggests that they joined in on the exodus. One commentator suggests that this group "might be foreigners living among Israel as temporary or long-term sojourners."[1] These people would likely in the future become aliens (*ger*) in early Israel.

So the reality is that from the earliest days the Israelites had to deal with the presence of aliens within their community. Furthermore, it is likely that when the Law was given at Mt. Sinai these non-Israelites were present. They would have known of the laws regarding the alien.

It might be recalled (see Chapter 3) that Moses' wife was a Midianite. While the story began with Moses being an alien in Midian, later on she would be considered as an outsider by some Israelites. In one of the instances where loving the alien was ignored, Aaron and Miriam, siblings of Moses, questioned Moses' supreme leadership by attacking his wife. While their purpose was to challenge Moses' status, they displayed some ugly racism. Numbers 12:1 opens this episode by reporting that "Miriam and Aaron began to talk against Moses because of his Cushite wife, for he had married a Cushite."

The identity of the Cushite wife has been a matter of scholarly debate over the centuries. Normally one expects a Cushite to be an African or Nubian from present-day Sudan or southern Egypt.[2] Thus some scholars believe this unnamed woman to be a different wife from Zipporah the Midianite, perhaps taken after his return to Egypt[3] or possibly from a marriage made in Egypt prior to his flight to Midian. The problem with this view is that this marriage is otherwise unattested in the Torah. Others favor equating the unnamed Cushite wife with Zipporah primarily since the Torah only describes this union and secondly because Cushan is used as an alternative term for Midian (cf. Hab. 3:7).[4] It is certain, however, that Miriam's objection is ethnically based.[5] For this bigotry, Miriam was divinely punished (Num. 12:9–12).

---

[1]William Propp, *Exodus 1–18, The Anchor Bible* (New York: Doubleday, 1998), 414.
[2]Gordon Wenham, *Numbers: An Introduction and Commentary* (Downers Grove, IL: InterVarsity Press, 1981), 110–111.
[3]Baruch Levine, *Numbers 1–20, The Anchor Bible* (New York: Doubleday, 1993), 328.
[4]James K. Hoffmeier, "Zipporah," in *International Standard Bible Encyclopedia*, IV (Grand Rapids, MI: Eerdmans, 1988), 1201.
[5]Jacob Milgrom, *Numbers: The JPS Torah Commentary* (Philadelphia: Jewish Publication Society, 1990), 93.

Regardless of which interpretation one follows, it is evident that some of Zipporah's family joined the Hebrews in Sinai and integrated into the new nation. As the Israelites were about to depart Sinai, Moses asked his in-laws to join him and promised that they could share in the Promised Land.

> Now Moses said to Hobab son of Reuel the Midianite, Moses' father-in-law, "We are setting out for the place about which the LORD said, 'I will give it to you.' *Come with us and we will treat you well*, for the LORD has promised good things to Israel."
>
> He answered, "No, I will not go; I am going back to my own land and my own people."
>
> But Moses said, "Please do not leave us. You know where we should camp in the desert, and you can be our eyes. *If you come with us, we will share with you whatever good things the LORD* gives us." (Num. 10:29–32)

From this exchange we learn how the Kenites, a Midianite clan, were invited to become aliens among the Israelites and to join in the blessings of the Promised Land. Hobab's initial response was to reject the offer, preferring to go back to his land (i.e., Midian) and live with his own people. While Numbers 10 does not include mention of the final response of the Kenites, Moses' second offer apparently worked. Saying no to an initial invitation of hospitality was (and remains) proper protocol in the Middle East.[6] We know that this clan joined the Israelites because centuries later the descendants of this family were still living among the Israelites, as the following narratives attest.

When the tribes were fighting for their possession in Canaan after the death of Joshua (Judg. 1:8–20), the Kenites, who were closely associated with Judah, settled in southern Canaan. "The descendants of Moses' father-in-law, the Kenite, went up from the City of Palms [viz. Jericho] with the men of Judah to live among the people of the Desert of Judah in the Negev near Arad" (Judg. 1:16). Probably due to their pastoral background, they chose to

[6]Victor Matthews and Don Benjamin, *Social World of Ancient Israel 1250–587 BCE* (Peabody, MA: Hendrickson, 1993), 82–83.

live in the region known for this lifestyle. A little later on they were found in northern Israel during the days of the judges Deborah and Barak: "Now Heber the Kenite had left the other Kenites, the descendants of Hobab, Moses' brother-in-law, and pitched his tent by the great tree in Zaanannim near Kedesh" (Judg. 4:11). In this tent, the Kenite Jael, a heroine, killed the Canaanite enemy general, Sisera (Judg. 4:16–23). Subsequently the Kenites are mentioned in connection with the activities of Kings Saul (1 Sam. 15:6) and David (1 Sam. 30:29). So they were very much a part of the community of Israel for centuries, and they retained their tent-dwelling lifestyle.

The narratives reviewed in this section reveal that from Israel's departure from Egypt, as well as during the Sinai wilderness period, Israel gathered to itself foreigners who became a part of the community and were classified as aliens. So before the tribes ever reached the Promised Land, aliens were included in the mix.

## THE ALIEN AND THE LAW OF DEUTERONOMY

Before his death in Trans-Jordan in the land of Moab, Moses conducted a ceremony in which the covenant made at Mt. Sinai (Exod. 20–24) was renewed. The idea of renewing the treaty with God was a key provision of ancient treaties, and the book of Deuteronomy actually specifies that the covenant should be regularly renewed by publically rereading it and the people recommitting themselves to its provisions:

> Then Moses commanded them: "*At the end of every seven years*, in the year for canceling debts, during the Feast of Tabernacles, *when all Israel* comes to appear before the LORD your God at the place he will choose, *you shall read this law before them in their hearing*." (Deut. 31:10–11)

The book of Deuteronomy in essence is the documentation of that renewal that includes the exposition of the Law given at Mt. Sinai by Moses (see Deut. 1:5ff.). The covenant had been ratified in Sinai forty years earlier, but the Torah is silent on whether aliens participated in that ceremony (Exod. 19–24). In the verses immediately following the instruction about the septennial renewal, we are explicitly told who should be included in the ritual when "all Israel" gathers for the Feast of Tabernacles.[7]

> Assemble the people—*men, women and children, and the aliens living in your towns*—so they can listen and learn to fear the LORD your God and follow carefully all the words of this law. Their children, who do not know this law, must hear it and learn to fear the LORD your God as long as you live in the land you are crossing the Jordan to possess. (Deut. 31:12–13)

The alien is included in this list, and as the second part of this passage indicates, the idea behind regular public reading of the Book of the Law is so the next generation would also hear it, learn it, and then abide by it. So not only is the alien included in this provision, but the focus shifts to the next generation so that they learn to reverence God. The result is that their children, including those of aliens, became further integrated into the faith of Israel. The alien, though not fully a citizen, was included in many of the blessings as well as the obligations of the covenant community, and as we saw in the previous chapter, the alien received all the legal protections, social benefits, and religious inclusion offered by the Law.

## ONCE IN THE LAND

Before his death in the Trans-Jordan, Moses was directed to have the people go to Mt. Ebal and Mt. Gerizim near Shechem to have a special ceremony (Deut. 11:29). This is actually reported as occurring after Joshua brought the people into the land of Canaan. The narrative reads:

> Then Joshua built on Mount Ebal an altar to the LORD, the God of Israel, as Moses the servant of the LORD had commanded the Israelites. He built it according to what is written in the Book of

[7]In Judaism, this festival is known by its Hebrew name, Succoth.

> the Law of Moses—an altar of uncut stones, on which no iron tool had been used. On it they offered to the LORD burnt offerings and sacrificed fellowship offerings. There, in the presence of the Israelites, *Joshua copied on stones the law of Moses*, which he had written. *All Israel, aliens and citizens alike*, with their elders, officials and judges, were standing on both sides of the ark of the covenant of the LORD, facing those who carried it—the priests, who were Levites. Half of the people stood in front of Mount Gerizim and half of them in front of Mount Ebal, as Moses the servant of the LORD had formerly commanded when he gave instructions to bless the people of Israel.
>
> Afterward, Joshua read all the words of the law—the blessings and the curses—just as it is written in the Book of the Law. There was not a word of all that Moses had commanded that Joshua did not read to *the whole assembly of Israel,* including the women and children, *and the aliens who lived among them.* (Josh. 8:30–35)

Some scholars now believe that the formal procedure described here was a land grant ceremony in which God was legally transferring the land to Israel.[8] In ancient Babylonia, specially inscribed land grant stones (called *kudurru*) were created to record the transfer of land from a ruler to a citizen. When Joshua followed the order of Moses to write a copy of the Law on a stone covered with plaster (Deut. 27:4) and "copied on stones the law of Moses" (Josh. 8:32), he apparently was making an Israelite form of a *kudurru* stone.

The Ebal ceremony described in Joshua 8, then, appears to be such a land grant, and as this momentous event was taking place, the text records, "aliens" were included in "all Israel" and in "the whole assembly." We may infer from this that a generation earlier, the parents of these aliens were part of the original mixed multitude who participated in the Sinai event. Others, like the Kenite-Midianites who joined subsequently, would also have witnessed the Ebal ceremony.

[8]Andrew Hill, "The Ebal Ceremony as Hebrew Land Grant?" *Journal of the Evangelical Theological Society*, 31, No. 4 (1988), 399–406.

Why were the aliens specifically included in this ceremony? The text does not offer a reason. The book of Joshua goes into great detail about the allocation of the territories tribe by tribe (13–19), but the aliens did not receive their own allotment. One possibility is that while they were not going to own property in any legal sense, they were going to live on the land and would benefit from it, especially the pastoralists whose flocks would graze in harvested fields and undeveloped land. And as we saw in our treatment of the Law, they did receive social benefits such as gleaning rights and a portion of the third-year tithes. Only as the ground produced grains and fruits would the Israelites and the aliens and their animals subsist. So in a very real sense they shared in the Promised Land.

## THE STORY OF RUTH

One of the most endearing stories in the Bible is that of Ruth, found in the book that bears her name. The protagonist was a Moabite woman who showed incredible loyalty to her widowed mother-in-law, and the story includes a beautiful romance! Set in the days when judges ruled Israel, several decades before Israel had a king, we are introduced to Elimelech and his wife Naomi, who were residents of Bethlehem in the tribal territory of Judah (Ruth 1:1–2). Hard times had struck Israel—drought and famine had taken its toll on the people. Elimelech decided to leave his home and the lands he owned and immigrated east across the Jordan River to the neighboring country of Moab. The NIV translation reads, "went to live for a while in the country of Moab" (1:1); other versions render it "went to sojourn" (e.g., KJV, RSV, ESV, NASB), which better communicates the intended meaning of the Hebrew term *gwr*, i.e., to live as aliens. This family moved due to the economic adversity, with the intent of making Moab their new home. The two sons even married Moabite women, Orpah and Ruth, indicating that they were integrating into Moabite society.

A short time later, unfortunately, tragedy hit the family again. First Elimelech died (1:3). Then about ten years later Naomi, the widow, lost her two sons (1:4–5), leaving her destitute with Orpah and Ruth as her only family. This was more than just a personal tragedy. As Lawson Younger puts it, "the family of Elimelech teeters on annihilation."[9] The annihilation of a family in ancient Israel was the ultimate social catastrophe.

Without a source of income, and with no hope of restoring her decimated family, Naomi decided to return to Israel. News reached Naomi that the famine that had driven them to become aliens in Moab had ended (1:6), which made the thought of returning home a more promising one.

The three women started the trip back to Bethlehem together, but then Naomi thought that her daughters-in-law might do better returning to their families and so urged them not to continue the journey back to Bethlehem (1:8). After much pleading back and forth, Orpah took Naomi's advice, but Ruth out of deep love and loyalty decided to stay with her mother-in-law and go to Israel (1:16–17).

Now their roles were reversed. Naomi who had been an alien in Moab was returning home, while Ruth was leaving her homeland to become an alien in Israel. But she pledged a new allegiance to Naomi and to the God of Israel when she vowed, "Your people will be my people and your God my God" (1:16). Thus Ruth, with Naomi as her host, went to Bethlehem as an alien.

Naomi the widow and Ruth the alien arrived in Israel just as the barley harvest was about to begin (Ruth 1:22). This would be in late April.[10] The two women certainly would be the type of individuals the Law intended to assist through the gleaning laws. Leviticus 19:9–10 and 23:22 specifies that the poor and the alien were eligible to take a portion of the grains from the fields when they were harvested, while Deuteronomy 24:19–21 adds "the alien, the fatherless and the widow." Knowing this, the elderly Naomi sent Ruth to the fields to obtain food to sustain them.

[9]K. Lawson Younger, *Judges/Ruth: The NIV Application Commentary* (Grand Rapids, MI: Zondervan, 2002), 417.
[10]Arthur Cundall and Leon Morris, *Judges & Ruth: An Introduction and Commentary* (Downers Grove, IL: InterVarsity Press, 1980), 263.

Providentially she ended up in the fields of a well-to-do relative (i.e., from the same clan), a man in the extended family of the deceased Elimelech named Boaz (Ruth 2:1–2). The kinsman took a special interest in Ruth, as he had heard of her loyalty to his relative Naomi, and offered her his protection while working, not to mention water to drink. Also, in effect he allowed her to gather more than he was obliged to let a gleaner take (Ruth 2:8–16). She was overwhelmed by his kindness, which led to the following exchange:

> At this, she bowed down with her face to the ground. She asked him, "*Why have I found such favor in your eyes that you notice me—a foreigner?*"
>
> Boaz replied, "I've been told all about what you have done for your mother-in-law since the death of your husband—*how you left your father and mother and your homeland and came to live with a people you did not know before*. May the LORD repay you for what you have done. May you be richly rewarded by the LORD, the God of Israel, under whose wings you have come to take refuge." (Ruth 2:10–12)

Obviously Ruth was surprised, if not staggered by the generous treatment she received. The gesture of bowing down is recognized as an expression of gratitude.[11] She is especially astonished because she, "a foreigner," was being treated so kindly. It is curious that she calls herself a "foreigner" (*nokheriah*, literally "a foreign woman") when she seems to fit the classic definition of an alien (*ger*). After all, Boaz acknowledged that she had left her land and family. Moreover, she had attached herself to a citizen through marriage to Elimelech's son and returned to Bethlehem with Naomi as her sponsor or host. Perhaps Ruth did not realize that in Israel, thanks to the special protective status of the alien in biblical law, she had a right to glean the fields. Alternatively, she may have used the term in a self-deprecating manner in order to accentuate the generosity of Boaz.

[11]Younger, *Judges/Ruth*, 444.

The story takes an intriguing twist when romance begins between Boaz and Ruth that leads to their marriage. By marrying Ruth and subsequently having children, Boaz restored the family of Elimelech and his sons.[12] He is what the Bible calls a "kinsman-redeemer" (*go'el*).

The story of Ruth is beautiful and touching, and it reveals informative details about Israelites who became aliens in neighboring Moab and how a Moabite alien woman was treated by the Israelites. But that is not why this book was written. As this gripping narrative ends, the purpose of the story is revealed in the final paragraphs of the book:

> Boaz took Ruth and she became his wife. Then he went to her, and the LORD enabled her to conceive, and she gave birth to a son. The women said to Naomi: "Praise be to the LORD, who this day has not left you without a kinsman-redeemer. May he become famous throughout Israel! He will renew your life and sustain you in your old age. For your daughter-in-law, who loves you and who is better to you than seven sons, has given him birth."
>
> Then Naomi took the child, laid him in her lap and cared for him. The women living there said, "Naomi has a son." And they named him Obed. He was the father of Jesse, the father of David.
>
> This, then, is the family line of Perez: Perez was the father of Hezron, Hezron the father of Ram, Ram the father of Amminadab, Amminadab the father of Nahshon, Nahshon the father of Salmon, Salmon the father of Boaz, Boaz the father of Obed, Obed the father of Jesse, and Jesse the father of David. (Ruth 4:13–22)

The great-grandson of Ruth and Boaz, as the genealogy reveals, turns out to be none other than Israel's greatest monarch, King David! It appears, then, that the purpose of this story is to show

---

[12]While Boaz clearly was romantically attracted to Ruth, he was also fulfilling a family obligation to his deceased relative, Elimelech, as proscribed by biblical law (cf. Deuteronomy 25:5–10). The technical term used for the practice of a brother or relative siring children for his deceased family member is levirate marriage; see Richard Kalmin, "Levirate Law," *Anchor Bible Dictionary*, 4, ed. D. N. Freedman (New York: Doubleday, 1992), 296–297.

how a Moabite alien married into the family of Elimelech, first through his son and then as a widow through Boaz, the kinsman-redeemer. And through this union this alien became an Israelite, thus eliminating any doubt that David's pedigree was legitimate because Deuteronomy 17:15 forbids a foreigner (*nakhri*) from becoming king. The story in essence serves to legitimize David by pointing out that Ruth was a true Israelite in terms of her faith and by virtue of her marriage.

## ALIENS IN THE DAYS OF KINGS SAUL, DAVID, AND SOLOMON

Reports mentioning aliens involved in the life of Israel are rather minimal during the period of Israel's monarchy. But there are some instructive references that shed further light on the status of aliens in Israel.

The tragic death of Israel's first king, Saul, occurred during a fierce battle with the Philistines (1 Sam. 31). When Saul realized the battle was lost and he would likely be captured, killed, and his remains desecrated, he asked his weapons-bearer to end his life with his sword (31:4). But the man refused, prompting the desperate king to fall on his own sword, thereby committing suicide. His loyal attendant followed suit (31:5).

News of the loss of the battle and the death of Saul and three of his sons was brought to David, who himself had been involved in military actions against the Amalekites, a nomadic people who had attacked and plundered David's stronghold at Ziklag in southern Israel (1 Sam. 30:1ff.). A messenger met David at Ziklag with the report of Saul's death. When David pressed him for details, the man, who identified himself as an Amalekite (2 Sam. 1:8), reported that he had seen the mortally wounded Saul during the battle (1:6–7) and that the king had begged the unnamed Amalekite to finish him off, which he claimed he did (1:9–10)! His story appears to be intentionally fabricated to curry favor with David.[13] When David demanded to know

[13]P. Kyle McCarter, *II Samuel*, *The Anchor Bible* (New York: Doubleday, 1984), 63.

where the man was from, he declared, "I am the son of an alien, an Amalekite" (1:13). He identifies himself as a *ger* rather than a foreigner (*nekhar*).

Based upon this declaration, it seems that despite the long history of animosity between Israel and the Amalekites (cf. Exod. 17; 1 Sam.15), this man's family had attained alien status, if he is to be believed. The nagging question is, what was this alien Amalekite doing in the field of battle so that he came upon Saul in the heat of the conflict? When the narrator introduces this alien Amalekite, he is called "a man" in some instances (2 Sam. 1:2) but more often is referred to as *na'ar* (2 Sam. 1:5, 6, 13), which is typically translated as "the young man" (e.g., NIV, RSV, KJV, JPS). This translation seems to obscure the identity of this "young man," and at first glance it appears to contradict that he is a male adult. The word *na'ar* has another meaning, however, one more appropriate to the context. Indeed in military settings the term is used of a young soldier,[14] and this is how the *Jerusalem Bible* has translated *na'ar* in this episode.

Accepting this meaning, it suggests that this alien was a soldier in Israel's army, which would explain what he was doing in the vicinity of King Saul when the battle was raging. The age for serving in the military was twenty (Num. 1:3). So either this alien was conscripted or had joined voluntarily. In either case, his role in the story and his identity as a *na'ar* suggests that aliens could serve in the military in ancient Israel. Similarly, aliens from various national backgrounds have volunteered in the U.S. military in recent decades.

The narrative of Saul's death opens a window that reveals that aliens could serve in Israel's army. Other passages from the period of the monarchy show additional areas in which aliens served the state. For example, when David began to organize materials and the workforce for the construction of the Temple in Jerusalem, a task actually undertaken and completed by his son Solomon, the chronicler offers this description:

[14]Ibid., 59.

> *So David gave orders to assemble the aliens living in Israel, and from among them he appointed stonecutters to prepare dressed stone for building the house of God.* He provided a large amount of iron to make nails for the doors of the gateways and for the fittings, and more bronze than could be weighed. He also provided more cedar logs than could be counted, for the Sidonians and Tyrians had brought large numbers of them to David. (1 Chron. 22:2–4)

Here aliens (*gerim*) are mentioned as being conscripted to work along with Israelites and other known skilled artisans. The "Sidonians and Tyrians," of course, are Phoenicians from present-day Lebanon, from which Solomon obtained building quality timber, including cedar and cypress, needed for the construction of the Temple. First Kings 5 contains the record of Solomon renewing the trade alliance David had had with the Phoenicians. Because Israel was deprived of good quality timber, this relationship with the Phoenicians was economically strategic for Israel. Additionally carpenters and stonemasons from Lebanon worked on this project, as 1 Chronicles indicates. A similar report is found in 1 Kings:

> King Solomon conscripted laborers from all Israel—thirty thousand men. He sent them off to Lebanon in shifts of ten thousand a month, so that they spent one month in Lebanon and two months at home. Adoniram was in charge of the forced labor. Solomon had seventy thousand carriers and eighty thousand stonecutters in the hills, well as thirty-three hundred overseers who supervised the project and directed the work. At the king's command they removed from the quarry large blocks of quality stone to provide a foundation of dressed stone for the temple. The craftsmen of Solomon and Hiram and those from Byblos [margin][15] cut and prepared the timber and stone for the building of the temple (5:13–18).

Israelites, aliens from within Israel, and Phoenicians were all involved in the work of the Temple construction. The inclu-

[15]Byblos is the port city in northern Lebanon from which logs were shipped to Egypt and Israel in ancient times.

sion of aliens suggests that they had particular skills in stone masonry like the Phoenicians and thus were very valuable to this endeavor. From the Iron II period (1000–722 B.C.), fine-quality carved limestone building blocks, called ashlars, were used in Israel. It was likely this kind of masonry that the aliens were cutting and shaping for the Temple.[16] Like the Israelites, aliens were also conscripted or drafted into this workforce to do grunt work. In order to find out how many aliens might be available to add to the workforce, Solomon took a census of the aliens to facilitate the conscription (2 Chron. 2:17). The total of aliens was a staggering 153,600. In 1 Kings 5 we find out that eighty thousand worked in the quarries moving stone, seventy thousand were assigned to bear burdens, and thirty-three hundred were appointed to be overseers.

At the dedication of Israel's first temple, its builder, Solomon, offered a lengthy prayer of dedication that included a section about the foreigner (*hanokheri*). He implored God as follows:

> As for *the foreigner* who does not belong to your people Israel but has come from a distant land because of your name—for men will hear of your great name and your mighty hand and your outstretched arm—when he comes and prays toward this temple, then hear from heaven, your dwelling place, and *do whatever the foreigner asks of you*, so that all peoples of the earth may know your name and fear you, as do your own people Israel, and may know that this house I have built bears your Name. (1 Kings 8:41–43)

This wonderful statement indicates that Solomon anticipated that foreigners would come a long distance for a pilgrimage to pray at the Jerusalem temple, and he wanted God to hear their prayers. People did indeed travel distances in the ancient world to go to various cult centers to bring petitions to deities in foreign lands. Solomon's prayer acknowledges this practice and believes that the reputation of Israel's God was such that people would hear about

[16]H. G. M. Williamson, *1 & 2 Chronicles, The New Century Bible Commentary* (Grand Rapids, MI: Eerdmans, 1982), 152–153.

him and come to pray. This openness to foreigners does not imply that such pilgrims would take up residency in Israel any more than pilgrims who go to Jerusalem or Rome today expect to become citizens.

A final mention of aliens in a historical setting occurs during the reign of the good king Hezekiah (715–686 B.C.). After a period of religious apostasy, Hezekiah introduced religious reforms and brought his nation into alignment with the stipulations of the Law. One of his crowning achievements was to celebrate Passover as a national event in Jerusalem. Here is a part of the Chronicler's description of that festive occasion:

> The whole assembly then agreed to celebrate the festival seven more days; so for another seven days they celebrated joyfully. Hezekiah king of Judah provided a thousand bulls and seven thousand sheep and goats for the assembly, and the officials provided them with a thousand bulls and ten thousand sheep and goats. A great number of priests consecrated themselves. The entire assembly of Judah rejoiced, along with the priests and Levites and all who had assembled from Israel, *including the aliens who had come from Israel and those who lived in Judah*. There was great joy in Jerusalem, for since the days of Solomon son of David king of Israel there had been nothing like this in Jerusalem. The priests and the Levites stood to bless the people, and God heard them, for their prayer reached heaven, his holy dwelling place. (2 Chron. 30:23–27)

Just as the Law allowed (see Chapter 4), the aliens were included in this celebrative throng. They participated in eating the Passover meal and received the priestly blessings that were extended to the people on that occasion.

The beauty of this story is that it shows that the religious inclusion intended for the alien was being taken seriously over five hundred years after the exodus from Egypt when the first aliens were permitted to join in the celebration of God's deliverance of Israel from bondage in Egypt (Exod. 12:19; Num. 9:14). The inclusion of the alien in the Passover illustrates that God wanted aliens to be recipients of his salvation, provided they followed the provisions laid out in the Law for their incorporation into the community of Israel. The story of Ruth certainly exemplifies this view. She not only came to Israel with a supporting host but openly confessed her faith in the God of Israel.

chapter 6

# LET JUSTICE ROLL: THE CHAMPIONS OF JUSTICE

**But let justice roll on like a river,**
**righteousness like a never-failing stream!**
**(Amos 5:24)**

The cry for justice by Israel's prophets is one of the recurring themes of the prophetic books of the Bible. When the eighth-century prophet Amos preached, "let justice roll on like a river, righteousness like a never-failing stream," he had no idea that this powerful declaration would become one of the most quoted passages from the Old Testament in the twentieth and twenty-first centuries. Many clergy and civil rights advocates cite these words to promote the cause of justice, especially social justice.

In fact, when I recently made a Google search of the phrase "let justice roll," I got 258,000 hits! The declaration by Amos was brought to the nation's attention in Dr. Martin Luther King Jr.'s "I have a dream" speech on August 28, 1963. He said, "No, no, we are not satisfied, and we will not be satisfied until 'justice rolls down like waters, and righteousness like a mighty stream.'" There is also a website with the address www.letjusticeroll.org. It belongs to a movement made up of more than ninety community groups and religious organizations that want to raise the minimum wage and champion a living wage for all citizens. *Let Justice Roll* is also the title of a book by John Perkins, the third edition of which was released in 2007. The uses of or appeals to this verse in recent years in North America are ubiquitous!

## THE PROPHETS AS CHAMPIONS OF JUSTICE

When the prophets expressed the heart of God to see justice in Israel, what did they mean, and how is that pertinent to the present day? First of all, when Israel's prophets called Israel's leaders and the people to justice, the standard for justice was none other than the Sinaitic covenant, the Law. This is because Moses, who was the mediator of the Law or covenant at Mt. Sinai, was also Israel's first national prophet.[1]

Toward the end of his life, he announced to the Israelites just prior to the entry into the Promised Land, "The LORD your God will raise up for you *a prophet like me* from among your own brothers. You must listen to him" (Deut. 18:15). Because of this statement and others, Moses is recognized as the prototype of the prophet in Israel, and this is why he is considered to be the "fountainhead of the prophetic tradition."[2] In addition, the kings of Israel were to base their kingship on the legal material in the Torah. In fact, Deuteronomy demands that the king have his own copy of the Law and read it!

> When he takes the throne of his kingdom, *he is to write for himself on a scroll a copy of this law*, taken from that of the priests, who are Levites. It is to be with him, and he is to read it all the days of his life so that he may learn to revere the LORD his God *and follow carefully all the words of this law and these decrees* and not consider himself better than his brothers and turn from the law to the right or to the left. Then he and his descendants will reign a long time over his kingdom in Israel. (Deut. 17:18–20)

Not only was the ruler to have a copy of the Law, he was to

[1]The word "prophet" (*navi'*) is actually first applied to Abraham (Gen. 20:7), but Moses plays a leadership role over the nation that makes him a unique prophet and leader.
[2]Willem VanGemeren, *Interpreting the Prophetic Word* (Grand Rapids, MI: Zondervan, 1990), 32.

live by it himself and not consider himself above the Law. The kings, moreover, would be assessed by their fidelity to the Law. King Hezekiah (715–687 B.C.), for example, received accolades for his faithfulness:

> Hezekiah trusted in the LORD, the God of Israel. There was no one like him among all the kings of Judah, either before him or after him. He held fast to the LORD and did not cease to follow him; *he kept the commands the LORD* had given Moses. (2 Kings 18:5–6)

When Hezekiah's son and successor, Manasseh (687–643 B.C.), did not follow his father's righteous ways but turned to pagan practices, the writer of 2 Kings declares that the king and his people were admonished to "be careful to do everything I commanded them" and to "keep the whole Law that my servant Moses gave them" (2 Kings 21:8). In the following verses, the author records that they ignored God's Law.

When the king of Judah failed to promote justice, Jeremiah actually went to the palace to confront the monarch, his officials, and the people.

> This is what the LORD says: "*Go down to the palace of the king of Judah and proclaim this message there*: 'Hear the word of the LORD, O king of Judah, you who sit on David's throne—you, your officials and your people who come through these gates. This is what the LORD says: *Do what is just and right. Rescue from the hand of his oppressor the one who has been robbed. Do no wrong or violence to the alien, the fatherless or the widow,* and do not shed innocent blood in this place. For if you are careful to carry out these commands, then kings who sit on David's throne will come through the gates of this palace, riding in chariots and on horses, accompanied by their officials and their people. *But if you do not obey these commands, declares the LORD*, I swear by myself that this palace will become a ruin.'" (Jer. 22:1–5)

Doing wrong and violence against the alien is included as

one of the crimes enumerated by the prophet in his indictment. Obedience to God's commandments was a condition of remaining in the Promised Land. The threat of the destruction of the land and exile hung over Israel!

The kings, then, were to uphold the Law and see that justice was done. When the king or nation deviated, the prophets swung into action. Consider the words of the late-seventh-century prophet Habakkuk who connects justice and the Law.

> *Why do you make me look at injustice?*
> *Why do you tolerate wrong?*
> *Destruction and violence are before me;*
> *there is strife, and conflict abounds.*
> *Therefore the law is paralyzed,*
> *and justice never prevails.*
> *The wicked hem in the righteous,*
> *so that justice is perverted. (1:3–4)*

In order to see that justice was upheld, the prophets became prosecutors who brought charges against the covenant people. Like a prosecutor in court, the prophets would enumerate the violations of the covenant stipulations, sometimes with specific details. Hence the echo of biblical law is heard in their preaching.

Jeremiah, the seventh–sixth-century prophet, proclaimed God's indictment when he was preaching at the entrance of the temple:

> *Will you steal and murder, commit adultery and perjury, burn incense to Baal and follow other gods you have not known,* and then come and stand before me in this house, which bears my Name, and say, "We are safe"—safe to do all these detestable things? Has this house, which bears my Name, become a den of robbers to you? But I have been watching! declares the LORD. (Jer. 7:9–11)

Notice that five of the Ten Commandments are cited or alluded to here. Earlier in the same sermon Jeremiah denounced the treatment of those most easily exploited when biblical justice is ignored:

> If you really change your ways and your actions and deal with each other justly, if you *do not oppress the alien, the fatherless or the widow* and do not shed innocent blood in this place, and if you do not follow other gods to your own harm, then I will let you live in this place, in the land I gave your forefathers for ever and ever. (Jer. 7:5–7)

Here the prophet in the same sentence decries those oppressing the alien, the fatherless, and the widow as well as those who murder (Sixth Commandment) and worship pagan deities (First and Second Commandments). The reference to the alien, the fatherless, and the widow, as we saw in Chapter 4, is treated in many places in the Law. Some of the laws specifically refer to the alien. For example:

> Do not mistreat an alien or oppress him, for you were aliens in Egypt. (Exod. 22:21)

> Do not oppress an alien; you yourselves know how it feels to be aliens, because you were aliens in Egypt. (Exod. 23:9)

In other passages, the same three categories of people are mentioned that Jeremiah cites, proving that his concern for justice for these poor folk is rooted in the Law itself. Consider Deuteronomy 10:17–18:

> For the LORD your God is God of gods and Lord of lords, the great God, mighty and awesome, who shows no partiality and accepts no bribes. *He defends the cause of the fatherless and the widow, and loves the alien*, giving him food and clothing.

While Jeremiah (7:5–7) speaks in general terms of oppressing the alien, he might be thinking about those who deny these needy people the right to glean from the fields and orchards at harvesttime. Once again the prophet is thinking of the laws of Deuteronomy:

> When you are harvesting in your field and you overlook a sheaf, do not go back to get it. *Leave it for the alien, the fatherless and the widow*, so that the LORD your God may bless you in all the work of your hands. When you beat the olives from your trees, do not go over the branches a second time. Leave what remains for *the alien, the fatherless and the widow*. When you harvest the grapes in your vineyard, do not go over the vines again. *Leave what remains for the alien, the fatherless and the widow.* Remember that you were slaves in Egypt. That is why I command you to do this. (Deut. 24:19–22)

In this last passage, even the sequence of alien, fatherless, and widow is the same as the one used by Jeremiah.

Other prophets also call attention to the same three groups of people. When the prophet Ezekiel, Jeremiah's contemporary, offers a rationale for the destruction of Jerusalem in 586 B.C., he calls it a "bloody city" (Ezek. 22:2, ESV, NASB, KJV, NKJV) and enumerates the violations of the Law. Verse 7 declares concerning the capital city:

> In you they have treated father and mother with contempt; in you they have *oppressed the alien and mistreated the fatherless and the widow*.

Then later in the same passage he adds:

> The people of the land practice extortion and commit robbery; they oppress the poor and needy and *mistreat the alien, denying them justice*. (Ezek. 22:29)

In both of these Ezekiel passages, the word "oppress" is used. This, however, is not the word for "oppress" (*lakhats*) that we encountered in some Torah passages. Rather in this case "oppress" (*'osheq*) can also mean "extortion"[3] and is found in

[3]KB, 897.

laws that deal with denying payment to workers (Lev. 19:13; Deut. 24:14). It seems clear enough that Ezekiel also has these laws from the Torah in mind. Actually *'osheq* occurs three times in verse 29, which in the first two instances are translated "practice extortion."[4] Thus the prophet is attacking the problem of either defrauding wages or extortion.[5] By treating the poor and the alien in this manner, justice (*mishpat*) was being denied. Here the oppressors are identified as "the people of the land," citizens and possibly landowners who have connections to or are supporters of the king.[6] Evidently these were people who had a degree of power and influence and were using their status and position to repress the disadvantaged.

In response to this behavior, the prophet condemns the violation of the Law against the alien because it was offensive to God, and now Jerusalem and its citizens would pay for this sin, along with a host of other offenses, with the doom of their land and deportation of most of the population (see Chapter 7 of this book). The prophets, then, were not just, as Hassell Bullock declares, "social reformers." Rather "they were theological reformers, for their basic motivation was generated within their commitment to the fundamental laws of God."[7]

## FAIR PAYMENT FOR WORK

Jeremiah again addresses the theme of exploiting workers by withholding wages or underpaying them in the days of King Jehoiakim (605–598 B.C.) of Judah.

> *Woe to him who builds his palace by unrighteousness,*
> *his upper rooms by injustice,*
> *making his countrymen work for nothing,*
> *not paying them for their labor (Jer. 22:13)*

[4]The Hebrew reads *'ashqu 'osheq*—the first occurrence is a verb followed by a noun.

[5]Andrew Hill, *Malachi, The Anchor Bible Commentary* (New York: Doubleday, 1998), 282.

[6]Daniel Block, *The Book of Ezekiel: Chapters 1–24* (Grand Rapids, MI: Eerdmans, 1997), 727.

[7]Hassell Bullock, *An Introduction to the Old Testament Prophetic Books* (Chicago: Moody Press, 1986), 25.

The use of the exclamatory prophetic word "woe" reveals divine anger at the injustice and the prospect of judgment on the unjust ruler.[8] In this case, the king was renovating his palace, making his residence more grand and luxurious. There is nothing wrong with that, but doing so and not paying the laborers violates the Law (Lev. 19:13; Deut. 24:14); hence the prophet denounces the legal violations and injustice. What is worse is that the king was supposed to be the exemplar and enforcer of justice, and yet he was the one depriving workers of their rightful earnings!

Jeremiah does not specifically identify aliens in his denunciation in Jeremiah 22:13, although some may have been included. The prophet Malachi (ca. 450 B.C.), however, does. He announces the day of God's judgment on evildoers when he will prosecute those who have violated his Law:

> Then I will draw near to you for judgment; I will be swift to bear witness against the sorcerers, against the adulterers, against those who swear falsely, *against those who oppress the hired workers in their wages*, the widow, and the orphan, *against those who thrust aside the alien*, and do not fear me, says the LORD of hosts. (Mal. 3:5, NRSV)

Here in the same indictment, divine judgment is pronounced on those who deprive (*'osheq*) laborers of their wages as well as those who deprive the alien. The expression "thrust aside" (*umatte*) is a bit obscure. "Thrust aside" from what? In some instances this verb is connected to the word *justice* (*mishpat*),[9] which is why the NIV renders this line as "deprive aliens of justice." Assuming this understanding, Malachi is expressing God's displeasure at those who deprive the alien of the justice that the Law stipulates for the *ger*. This general statement certainly includes payment for labor.

The fact that the Hebrew prophets specifically decried the behavior of employers who deprived workers of their rightful earnings, including the alien, demonstrates that the Law was to be

[8]Ronald Clements, "Woe," *Anchor Bible Dictionary*, 6, ed. D. N. Freedman (New York: Doubleday, 1992), 945–946.
[9]Hill, *Malachi*, 283–284.

taken seriously and that the prophets sought to come to the aid of those who were financially strapped by such abuse and to correct the situation.

The issue of properly paying one's employees is also taken up in the New Testament and is placed in the context of what James calls "the royal law"—"If you really keep the royal law found in Scripture, 'Love your neighbor as yourself,' you are doing right" (Jas. 2:8). Here, of course, James is quoting the famous passage from Leviticus 19:18 cited previously. It has been observed that he is "deeply influenced by Leviticus 19," which, John Hartley notes, is in turn "filtered through the teaching of Jesus. The central ethical precept is to love one's neighbor as oneself."[10] An example of failing to live up to this ethic is the treatment of employees, a subject James addresses in 5:1–4:

> Now listen, you rich people, weep and wail because of the misery that is coming on you. Your wealth has rotted, and moths have eaten your clothes. Your gold and silver are corroded. Their corrosion will testify against you and eat your flesh like fire. You have hoarded wealth in the last days. *Look! The wages you failed to pay the workers who mowed your fields are crying out against you. The cries of the harvesters have reached the ears of the Lord Almighty.*

Hoarding wealth is what drives the callous behavior of the rich people being indicted here.[11] While the Deuteronomy passage declares that the violated worker would cry out for justice, James has both the worker and the money robbed from the work crying out for redress.

It is not insignificant that both Testaments address the wrong of depriving or defrauding workers of their pay. The Bible plainly takes this offense seriously and includes the alien as one who should not be victimized by unscrupulous and unethical employers who care only about increasing their profit margin. Sadly, many

---

[10]John Hartley, *Leviticus 1–27* (Dallas: Word, 1992), 335.
[11]Donald W. Burdick, "James," in *The Expositor's Bible Commentary*, Vol. 12, ed. Frank E. Gaebelein (Grand Rapids, MI: Zondervan, 1981), 200.

business owners and managers are guilty today of this very offense. People of conscience should be able to agree that our legal system should punish those who underpay or deprive of benefits any worker, including the alien, who might be the last one to complain or file a grievance.

## CONCLUSION

The prophets of Israel indeed were champions of justice, and God's standard of justice was rooted in the Torah. That was the measuring stick they used. According to the Torah, fear of and love for God was characterized by obedience to the old laws of Sinai (Deut. 10:12–13; 11:13; 13:4). This was at the heart of the message of the prophets, and the laws regarding the alien were a vital part of the Law. So the prophets were not pointing the people of Israel in a new or different direction (or definition) of social justice but to an old and familiar—but sadly neglected—path found in the Law. Jeremiah put it this way:

> *Stand at the crossroads and look;*
> *ask for the ancient paths,*
> *ask where the good way is, and walk in it,*
> *and you will find rest for your souls. (Jer. 6:16)*

Invariably, that path requires correcting violations of the Law, be they moral or social. Isaiah records God's demands as follows:

> *Take your evil deeds out of my sight!*
> *Stop doing wrong, learn to do right!*
> *Seek justice, encourage the oppressed.*
> *Defend the cause of the fatherless,*
> *plead the case of the widow. (Isa. 1:16–17)*

chapter 7

# BY THE RIVERS OF BABYLON

**By the rivers of Babylon we sat and wept when we remembered Zion. (Ps. 137:1)**

After Solomon's death in 931 B.C., his kingdom was split in two, with the Davidic kings ruling from Jerusalem over the kingdom of Judah. The northern part of the nation was ruled by Jeroboam I and his successors, and that kingdom was known as Israel. After two hundred years, Israel was destroyed by the Assyrians from northern Iraq, and a sizable portion of the population was deported to Assyria and Media (northern Iran) (2 Kings 17:5–6). During the period of Assyrian hegemony over Israel, Judah too experienced attacks and deportations (2 Kings 18:13–18). In Assyrian records, King Sennacherib boasts of removing tens of thousands of people and animals as booty: "I took 200,150 people, donkeys, camels, cattle, and sheep, without number."[1] Thus by 700 B.C. there were thousands of Israelites scattered across the lands east of the Holy Land living in exile. But it did not stop with the Assyrians.

The darkest hours for ancient Israel as a people were surely when Jerusalem was destroyed in 586 B.C., followed by the deportation of a significant percentage of the population to Babylon by King Nebuchadnezzar (2 Kings 25:1–21). The calamities began in

[1]Mordechai Cogan, in *Context of Scripture*, II, eds. W. W. Hallo and K. L. Younger (Leiden: Brill, 2000), 303.

605 B.C. when the recently crowned Nebuchadnezzar advanced on Judah and Jerusalem, making it a vassal state (2 Kings 24:1). On that occasion, the king took a select group of deportees whom he intended to educate and train for three years in Babylon, apparently so they could be civil servants back in Judah (Dan. 1:3–4). Daniel, the statesman-prophet, was one of these young men (Dan. 1:6).

Subsequently, King Jehoiakim in Jerusalem rebelled against Nebuchadnezzar, which brought swift retaliation from Babylon. In the intervening months, Jehoiakim died and was succeeded by his eighteen-year-old son Jehoiachin (2 Kings 24:1–8), who had to face the ire of the emperor. In 597 B.C. the young king was deported, along with a number of other members of royalty, high-ranking officials, seven thousand soldiers, and a thousand artisans (2 Kings 24:10–16). As a consequence, more than ten thousand Jews found themselves in Babylonia, and more would follow.

A decade later the last of the Davidic rulers, Zedekiah, likewise rebelled against Nebuchadnezzar, precipitating yet another invasion from Babylon (2 Kings 24:20b; 25:1–7). This time Jerusalem was sacked, and the palace and temple burnt, with most of its sacred utensils taken as plunder. Additionally the king and thousands more were exiled to Mesopotamia.

> On the seventh day of the fifth month, in the nineteenth year of Nebuchadnezzar king of Babylon, Nebuzaradan commander of the imperial guard, an official of the king of Babylon, came to Jerusalem. He set fire to the temple of the LORD, the royal palace and all the houses of Jerusalem. Every important building he burned down. The whole Babylonian army, under the commander of the imperial guard, broke down the walls around Jerusalem. *Nebuzaradan the commander of the guard carried into exile the people who remained in the city, along with the rest of the populace and those who had gone over to the king of Babylon.* But the commander left behind some of the poorest people of the land to work the vineyards and fields. (2 Kings 25:8–12)

From 605 to 539 B.C., when the exile officially ended, tens

of thousands of Jews were forced to live in a foreign land about nine hundred miles from Jerusalem.[2] Psalm 137:1–4 expresses the national mood:

> By the rivers of Babylon we sat and wept
> when we remembered Zion.
> There on the poplars
> we hung our harps,
> for there our captors asked us for songs,
> our tormentors demanded songs of joy;
> they said, "Sing us one of the songs of Zion!"
> *How can we sing the songs of the* LORD
> *while in a foreign land?*

In Babylon the Jews wept when they thought of their homeland. The loss of their land, the termination of the kingship, and the desecration of the Temple was a national humiliation, and the exile period has been described as "the most traumatic in the nation's history."[3]

What is intriguing about the period of the Assyrian and Babylonian captivities is that the Jews are never called aliens (*gerim*), and neither is the verb "to sojourn" nor "to live as an alien" (*gwr*) ever used in the Hebrew writings that treat the exile period. Rather they are called "exiles" (*golah* or *goluth*), and they were "exiled" (*hegelah*) to Babylon (see, e.g., 2 Kings 17:23; Jer. 24:5; 28:4, 6; 29:1, 4; Ezek. 1:1–2; 3:11, 15; 25:3; Dan. 2:25; 5:13). So the verb "to exile" and the noun "exiles" are consistently used to describe what happened to the nation and to the people themselves. One might naturally ask why they were labeled exiles and not aliens. Were they not residing in a foreign land? True, the Jews were living in a distant alien land, but they had been taken to Mesopotamia by force; they were prisoners of war. As we have seen (Chapter 2), an alien in ancient Israel (*ger*) was one who resided

[2]This distance reflects the travel route between Babylon and Judah, that is, north along the Euphrates, west into Syria, and then south to Israel. The direct distance, as the crow flies, between the two is much less, but it was entirely a desert track and was not used for travel between Mesopotamia and the Levant.
[3]*NIDOTTE*, 861.

in a foreign land by choice with the permission of the host nation. Furthermore, it was noted that aliens considered the land of their sojourning to be their new home. As Psalm 137 emphasizes, the Jewish exiles longed to return to their homeland, Judah.

## LIFE DURING THE BABYLONIAN EXILE

Despite the fact that the seventy-year exile marked a period of humiliation for Israel, and what they suffered was likened to their bondage in and exodus from Egypt (cf. Jer. 16:14–15; 23:7–8; Ezek. 20:36–37), we know very little about their life experience in Babylon. Jeremiah the prophet was active during the period between 597–586 B.C., and in the book that bears his name portions of several letters between himself and the exiles in Babylon are included. These offer a glimpse at the conditions of the Jews in Babylon, and from them we see that the prophet encouraged them to live constructive lives as captives in a foreign land.

> This is the text of the letter that the prophet Jeremiah sent from Jerusalem to the surviving elders among the exiles and to the priests, the prophets and all the other people Nebuchadnezzar had carried into exile from Jerusalem to Babylon. . . .
>
> This is what the LORD Almighty, the God of Israel, says to all those I carried into exile from Jerusalem to Babylon: "*Build houses and settle down; plant gardens and eat what they produce. Marry and have sons and daughters; find wives for your sons and give your daughters in marriage, so that they too may have sons and daughters*. Increase in number there; do not decrease. Also, *seek the peace and prosperity of the city to which I have carried you into exile. Pray to the LORD* for it, because if it prospers, you too will prosper." (Jer. 29:1, 4–7)

The contents of this letter are illuminating in several areas. First, it reveals that even though the Jews were in captivity, they had a degree of freedom. They could build homes and plant gardens and could freely marry and have children. This description makes it clear that the Jews during this period were not living in concentration camps or in prisons. More significantly, Jeremiah's letter encouraged the people to take a very positive attitude toward the land by settling in it and working for "the peace and prosperity of the city to which I have carried you into exile." Instead of rebelling against the Babylonian state, which is implied here,[4] the exiles are encouraged to promote "peace and prosperity" (*shalom*) in Babylon, and they were to pray to God for its well-being (*shalom*).

Good biblical role models of the philosophy advocated by Jeremiah are found in Joseph and Daniel. The former, as we saw previously, was sold by family members in Canaan and was taken to Egypt where he was bought by an Egyptian master. Joseph through his hard work and integrity made his master prosper (Gen. 39), but he used his influence and divinely given ability to prepare Egypt for a famine that affected the whole region. Not only did Egypt prosper through Joseph's agency, but so did neighboring peoples and even his own family in Canaan (Gen. 40–45).

The book of Daniel contains the story of a young man who had as a youth been taken to Babylon against his will and was forced to learn the Babylonian language and literature (Dan. 1:4, 6). Rather than opposing his situation or through passive aggression seeking to foil the plan of Nebuchadnezzar, Daniel worked diligently and succeeded. He made lemonade out of the lemons he had been handed! Subsequently Daniel was placed in high positions within the administration. By the end of his life he was elevated to the position of third ruler in the kingdom of Babylon (Dan. 5:29). He was also promoted to influential posts under the Persians (Dan. 6:1–3). Some later traditions claim that Daniel used his influence on the Persian emperor Cyrus to release the Jews from Babylon and to support the rebuilding of the Temple. We don't know if this is true or not, but it is certainly plausible. The point remains that Daniel followed the prudent course of working in a positive and constructive manner from which he personally benefited, but he

[4]William Holladay, *A Commentary of the Book of the Prophet Jeremiah Chapters 26–52* (Minneapolis: Fortress Press, 1989), 141.

also contributed to the *shalom* of his colleagues in the court and of his people as well.

Even though the Jewish exiles had every reason to be negative detractors of their new status quo, the divine message is just the opposite. Obviously as Babylon prospered, the benefits would overflow to the exilic community. It is hard to see any direct relevance of the doctrine of these passages to the North American scene. Those who were shipped to the West as slaves might be the closest analogy. Those who immigrate to America or Canada today, however, do so voluntarily. Nevertheless, it is certainly true that immigrants to any country should follow the advice of Jeremiah's letter (as should citizens). They should work hard and be constructive, thereby promoting the *shalom* of their new homeland, because as it flourishes, so will they. A second point from Jeremiah's message is that aliens should avoid social and political insurrection.

## TOWARD THE NEW TESTAMENT

With the demise of the Babylonian empire and the rise of the Persians over the world of the Bible, the captive Jews were permitted to return to Judah and Jerusalem and rebuild their lives, homes, and temple (Ezra 1–6). Life was not easy for the returnees, and many Jews opted to stay in Mesopotamia, as we learn from the lives and examples of Ezra, Nehemiah, Mordecai, and Esther. The Persians dominated the Mediterranean world from toward the end of the sixth century B.C. and for the next three centuries, and yet several of their emperors (Cyrus, Darius, and Artaxerxes) provided legal and economic assistance to the Jews in their efforts to be repatriated and to reconstruct Jerusalem. It may well be that because leaders like Daniel, Ezra, Nehemiah, and Esther followed Jeremiah's advice to "seek the peace and prosperity" of the land of their exile, that resulted in the favorable treatment of the Jews by these Persian emperors after their conquest of Babylon in 539 B.C.

Before the fourth century ended, Alexander the Great tipped

the balance of power in his favor, and Greek political and cultural hegemony spread through the biblical world. Another major political shift occurred in 63 B.C. when Rome took control of the Holy Land. And it is the Roman-controlled Mediterranean shaped by Greek or Hellenistic culture that is the world of the New Testament.[5]

[5]For a review of the history of the period of the Babylonian exile to the Roman period in the Holy Land, see James K. Hoffmeier, *The Archaeology of the Bible* (Oxford: Lion Hudson, 2008), Chapters 9–10.

chapter 8

# JESUS AND THE NEW TESTAMENT

**[Y]ou are no longer foreigners and aliens, but fellow citizens with God's people and members of God's household. (Eph. 2:19)**

Readers of the Bible may be surprised to learn that the New Testament offers no direct teaching or law about aliens and the illegal immigrant to guide a nation that is trying to resolve the thorny ethical or legal issues facing most western countries today. That is not to say that reports of immigrants and refugees are not contained therein, but there are good reasons, as we shall see in this chapter, for the relative silence of the New Testament on the matter.

## JESUS THE REFUGEE

One celebrated New Testament refugee and alien in a foreign land was Jesus Christ himself. The Gospel of Matthew begins with the narrative of the events surrounding the birth of Jesus of Nazareth (Matt. 1:18–25; 2; cf. Luke 1–2). One of the iconic images of the account is the coming of wise men from the east who followed a mysterious star they believed heralded the birth of a new king. After the magi visited the Christ-child in Bethlehem, they decided not to return to King Herod, who had demanded a report on the whereabouts of the Christ-child. Consequently the paranoid ruler unleashed a diabolical campaign to kill all the male infants in the area of Bethlehem who were under two (Matt. 2:1–16). He could not tolerate the thought of the birth of a king who might challenge his sovereignty or dynasty! A divine warning in a dream instructed Joseph to take little Jesus and Mary and flee to Egypt to spare the boy's life (2:13).

What is forgotten about this familiar story is that for a period of several years, Joseph, Mary, and Jesus were themselves refugees in Egypt. The Gospels pass over this segment of the life of Jesus in silence. We do not know under what circumstances they entered Egypt and where the Holy Family lived. According to Coptic Orthodox Christian tradition in Egypt, they moved throughout the land, and today a number of churches mark the locations where tradition claims they sojourned.

It is likely that the Holy Family would have traveled overland across North Sinai along the sand dune-laced ancient route that connected Egypt and Israel. This ancient road had varied little over the millennia.[1] As they approached the Egyptian frontier, they would have certainly been confronted by a series of imposing forts that functioned under Roman military authority (see next section on Roman rule). Some of these have been uncovered in the past twenty years. Pelusium was the strategic maritime entry port on the Mediterranean coast. According to an ancient Roman itinerary, a fortified sight named Magdala was located southwest of Pelusium. This site has long been identified with Tell el-Herr. It was perched on the eastern edge of an ancient marshy lake or lagoon. Excavations over the past two decades there have revealed two forts that span from the Persian through Roman periods (see Figure 10).[2] The next post along the road into Egypt was at Tell Abu Sefeh, about nine miles further east. Here another large Roman fort with large round bastions was unearthed in the 1990s. The defense walls were about twenty feet thick and measured 520 by 325 feet (see Figures 11a, 11b).[3]

[1]Pau Figueras, *From Gaza to Pelusium: Materials for the Historical Geography of North Sinai and Southwestern Palestine (332 BCE– 640 CE)* (Beer-Sheva: Ben-Gurion University of the Negev Press, 2000).

[2]Dominique Valbelle, "The First Persian Period Fortress at Tell El-Herr," *Egyptian Archaeology*, 18 (2001), 12–14.

[3]Peter Grossman, et. al., "The Roman Castrum of Tell Abu Sayfi at Qantara," *Mitteilunger des Deutschen Archäologischen Instituts Abteilung Kairo*, 53 (1997), 221–226.

**FIGURE 10**

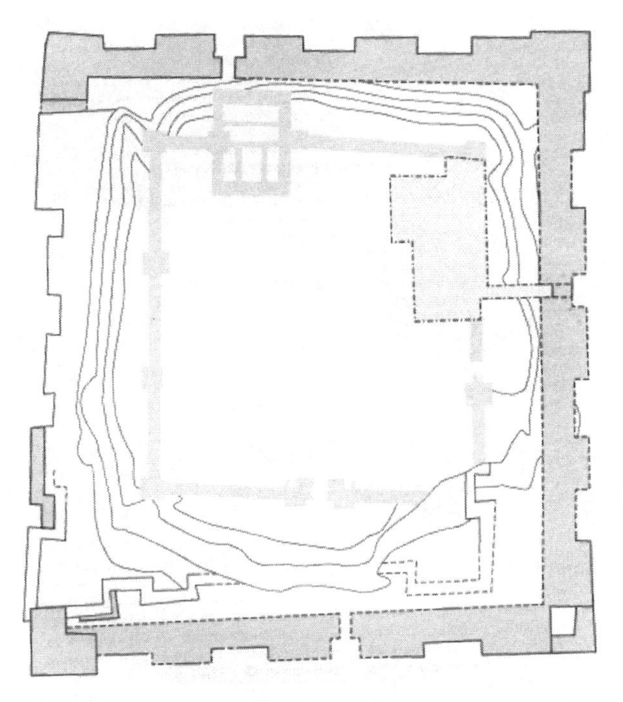

Plan of Greco-Roman Period Fort at Tell el-Herr, N. Sinai. (D. Valbell & G. Nogara, "La Forresse du Ive siècle avant J.-C. à Tell el-Herr (Nord-Sinai).

At one of these military stations, Joseph undoubtedly had to stop and obtain permission to enter Egypt. Perhaps he used his trade as a carpenter to get in and look for work. At this time there was a significant population of Jews in Egypt. Philo of Alexandria, the Jewish philosopher and theologian, lived in Egypt until A.D. 50 and claimed a million Jews were there at that time. Modern historians think this number is too high, but it certainly demonstrates that there was a large Jewish community in which the Holy Family could seek assistance, shelter, and employment during their brief stay. The reality is, we don't know what happened in Egypt, but it is evident that for a period of a few years Jesus and his family were refugees, aliens in Egypt.

**FIGURE 11a**

Large administrative building within the fort, Tell Abu Sefeh, N. Sinai.

**FIGURE 11b**

Roman period fort, SW Bastion at Tell Abu Sefeh, N. Sinai.

Despite this episode in his life, Jesus never directly spoke about aliens or refugees and how they should be treated. In fact, the New Testament is conspicuously silent on the matter.

## THE WORLD OF THE NEW TESTAMENT

Given the impressive amount of information about aliens in the Old Testament and how they were to be treated in ancient Israel, one might think this emphasis would carry over into the Gospels and epistles in the New Testament, but surprisingly this is not the case. To be sure, the teachings of Jesus and the books of other New Testament writers have much to say about how people ought to be treated. However, there is no direct instruction about the alien. There are good reasons for this silence.

First of all, the Jews and earliest Christians no longer lived in an independent nation. Rather, Judea and Galilee existed under the domination of Rome. The birth narratives of Jesus in the Gospel of Luke can be recited by nearly everyone in the English-speaking world because we hear the words regularly during the Christmas season in church services, in personal readings, and even in Charlie Brown's Christmas TV special. They begin by establishing the historical setting of the life of Christ and the New Testament.

> In those days Caesar Augustus issued a decree that a census should be taken of the entire Roman world. (This was the first census that took place while Quirinius was governor of Syria.) And everyone went to his own town to register. (Luke 2:1–3)

Caesar Augustus (43 B.C.–A.D. 14), whose name was Octavian, ruled the entire eastern Mediterranean world, including the Holy Land, and that continued throughout the entire period covered by the New Testament and for the next several centuries. While the Jews in the Holy Land were granted a fair degree of freedom, especially in religious practices and social laws, Roman law was the law of the land. Caesar made decrees and laws that subject states had to follow. Even the kings of the Jews, such as Herod the Great and his descendants, were appointees of Rome, and Caesar's governors, such as Quirinius, Pontius Pilate, Felix, and Festus, ensured that the Emperor's policies were enforced, that taxes were collected and security maintained. As a consequence, most of the issues facing the Jewish community during the first centuries A.D. and facing Christians too involved how to live as subjects of Rome while being good Jews or Christians.

The second reason for the absence of legal and social laws regarding the alien in the New Testament is that Christians did not occupy or control a nation or territory with clearly delineated borders like ancient Israel did in Old Testament times. Rather, communities of Christians (churches) were scattered throughout the Roman world; hence they viewed themselves as aliens in this world and citizens of the kingdom of God.

## THE KINGDOM OF GOD

The thrust of the preaching of Jesus and his disciples focused on the proclamation of the gospel or "good news" about the kingdom of God. At the outset of Mark's Gospel we are informed that "Jesus went into Galilee, proclaiming the good news of God. 'The time has come,' he said. 'The kingdom of God is near. Repent and believe the good news!'" (1:14–15).

On another occasion Jesus is recorded as saying, "I must preach the good news of the kingdom of God to the other towns also, because that is why I was sent" (Luke 4:43). The expression *kingdom of God* occurs more than sixty times in the New Testament. The kingdom of God occupies a central place in the New Testament, and one theologian, John Bright, thought it was the unifying theme of the entire Bible.[4]

A variant expression of *kingdom of God* is *kingdom of heaven*,[5] which is found more than thirty times in the New Testament. Its use reflects the spiritual nature of this kingdom. On

[4]John Bright, *The Kingdom of God: The Biblical Concept and Its Meaning for the Church* (Nashville: Abingdon-Cokesbury, 1953).
[5]G. E. Ladd, "Kingdom of Christ, God, Heaven," in *Evangelical Dictionary of Theology*, ed. Walter A. Elwell (Grand Rapids, MI: Baker, 2001), 607. An even shorter alternative is simply *the kingdom*.

the one hand, the New Testament teaches that the kingdom of God was initiated with the coming of Jesus himself (Matt. 12:28), while on the other hand it will not be fully realized and will not come until the end of human history (Mark 14:25; Luke 22:16, 18). The kingdom of God is a spiritual kingdom into which one enters as a result of a spiritual rebirth (John 3:3–5).

One of the charges brought against Jesus at his trial before Pilate was that he claimed to be a king, a charge that led to the following exchange:

> Pilate then went back inside the palace, summoned Jesus and asked him, "Are you the king of the Jews?"
>
> "Is that your own idea," Jesus asked, "or did others talk to you about me?"
>
> "Am I a Jew?" Pilate replied. "It was your people and your chief priests who handed you over to me. What is it you have done?"
>
> Jesus said, "*My kingdom is not of this world. If it were, my servants would fight to prevent my arrest by the Jews. But now my kingdom is from another place.*" (John 18:33–36)

The response of Jesus reveals his understanding that his kingdom, the kingdom of God or heaven, which he had been proclaiming for the previous two to three years, was not an earthly, full-bloomed present reality. It certainly was not represented by any geopolitical entity. Because Christians are a part of a yet—not yet kingdom, they remain outsiders in the world. Hence they were aliens in the eyes of the writers of the New Testament, as the next section reveals.

## CHRISTIANS AS ALIENS

Like Israelites of old who lived as aliens in Egypt and experienced mistreatment and abuse, Christians are aliens in this world, with no earthly homeland. Rather, as the book of Hebrews frames it, the Christian, like Abraham, is ultimately a sojourner or alien and not a citizen of any country.

> By faith Abraham, when called to go to a place he would later receive as his inheritance, obeyed and went, even though he did not know where he was going. By faith *he made his home in the promised land like a stranger in a foreign country; he lived in tents*, as did Isaac and Jacob, who were heirs with him of the same promise. For he was looking forward to the city with foundations, whose architect and builder is God. (Heb. 11:8–10)

Then, reflecting on the ancestors of Israel in Genesis, Hebrews 11 concludes:

> All these people were still living by faith when they died. They did not receive the things promised; they only saw them and welcomed them from a distance. And they admitted that they were *aliens and strangers* on earth. People who say such things show that they are looking for a country of their own. If they had been thinking of the country they had left, they would have had opportunity to return. Instead, *they were longing for a better country—a heavenly one*. Therefore God is not ashamed to be called their God, for he has prepared a city for them. (vv. 13–16)

The Greek words rendered for "he made his home" (v. 9) is *parokesen*, meaning "live as a sojourner,"[6] while the words "aliens and strangers" (v. 13) are *xenoi* and *parepidemoi*. The former indeed means alien or foreigner but also "wanderer, stranger, refugee" and is sometimes used synonymously with *paraikos*.[7] These Greek words are in fact among the terms used when the Hebrew Bible was translated into Greek during the third century B.C. in the so-called Septuagint in passages like Genesis 23:4 and 47:4. It was noted previously (in Chapter 4) that the Greek word *proselytos*, meaning "proselyte" or "convert," is another translation for *ger* in religious contexts.[8] Because the New Testament writers use Old Testament characters to illustrate the comparison

[6] F. F. Bruce, The *Epistle to the Hebrews* (Grand Rapids, MI: Eerdmans, 1964), 296, n. 82.
[7] Gerhard Friedrich, ed., *Theological Dictionary of the New Testament*, V (Grand Rapids, MI: Eerdmans, 1967), 1–2.
[8] "Proselyte," in *Anchor Bible Dictionary*, 5, ed. D. N. Freedman (New York: Doubleday, 1992), 503.

between the Christian and the sojourning Genesis ancestors of Israel, they are likely using these terms with the same meanings in mind (see discussion of the Hebrew terms in Chapter 2 of this book). Abraham and his descendants lived as aliens in Canaan and Egypt, and the Christians were to view themselves similarly.

The idea that Christians are aliens and that their ultimate citizenship is not in this world is further reflected in the writings of Peter. His first epistle opens by addressing his audience as "God's elect, *strangers in the world*, scattered throughout Pontus, Galatia, Cappadocia, Asia and Bithynia" (1 Pet. 1:1). Alternatively, "aliens of the *diaspora*" is a fitting translation for *parepidemoi*.[9] Later on Peter addresses his audience as "aliens and strangers in the world" (*paroikous* and *parepidemous*, 1 Pet. 2:11). This language is intentionally used, I. Howard Marshall maintains, to show that like the Jews who were scattered around the world and living outside their homeland, Christians are aliens in the world because of their status as citizens of the kingdom of God.[10]

At the same time, because the Christian is viewed as a citizen of the kingdom of God, Paul tells the believers in Ephesus, "you are no longer foreigners and aliens, but fellow citizens with God's people and members of God's household" (Eph. 2:19). So the New Testament regards Christians as being aliens in this world, but not aliens with respect to their relationship with God; rather they are members of the family of faith.

Consequently, the main reason the New Testament does not address the question of aliens in the same way that the Old Testament law does is because Christians in the first century were the aliens who had no homeland, and like the patriarchs of Genesis, "they were longing for a better country—a heavenly one" (Heb. 11:16). Christians, then, find themselves in the paradoxical situation of being citizens of a heavenly kingdom and yet living in different earthly states, each with its own laws and requirements. How does one cope with this dual citizenship?

[9]The Greek word in 1 Peter 1:1 is *diaspora*.
[10]I. Howard Marshall, *1 Peter* (Downers Grove, IL: InterVarsity Press, 1991), 30.

## CHURCH VERSUS STATE

Christians have long wrestled with the relationship between church and state or between faith and the practice of one's faith-based convictions as a citizen of a secular nation.[11] In a sense Jesus addressed this question directly when asked about whether he, a Jew, approved of paying taxes to the oppressive Roman government that exercised hegemony over the Holy Land. This insightful interaction followed the question:

> "Is it right to pay taxes to Caesar or not? Should we pay or shouldn't we?"
>
> But Jesus knew their hypocrisy. "Why are you trying to trap me?" he asked. "Bring me a denarius and let me look at it." They brought the coin, and he asked them, "Whose portrait is this? And whose inscription?"
>
> "Caesar's," they replied.
>
> Then Jesus said to them, "Give to Caesar what is Caesar's and to God what is God's." (Mark 12:14d–17a; cf. Luke 20:21–25)

The purpose behind the question of the opponents of Jesus was to create a quandary for him. Side with Caesar and he would alienate the Jewish authorities and his followers; go against Rome and he could be charged with treason. When Jesus answered, "Give to Caesar what is Caesar's and to God what is God's," he demonstrated that one does not have to pit the earthly ruler against God. He also illustrated that "there are obligations to Caesar which do not infringe the rights of God but are indeed ordained by God."[12] Jesus thus was teaching an important principle, namely, that supporting the government is a God-ordained duty.[13] The late William Lane explained the implications of Jesus' teaching this way: "There are obligations to the state which

---

[11]For a recent treatment of this issue from different theological and ecclesiastical traditions, see P. C. Kemeny, ed., *Church, State and Public Justice: Five Views* (Downers Grove, IL: InterVarsity Press, 2007).

[12]C.E.B Cranfield, *The Gospel According to Saint Mark* (Cambridge: Cambridge University Press, 1959), 372.

[13]Walter Liefeld, *Luke, The Expositors Bible Commentary*, 8 (Grand Rapids, MI: Zondervan, 1984), 1016.

do not infringe on the rights of God but are grounded in his appointment."[14]

While it may be a bitter pill to swallow for democratic-minded westerners or political partisans who think the voting majority determines who the political leaders will be, Scripture maintains that God is the one who raises up leaders and removes them (cf. Daniel 2:36–48). This is true of noble kings and vile dictators, as well as presidents and prime ministers in democracies. Jesus himself confirmed this view when being tried by the Roman governor, Pontius Pilate:

> When Pilate heard this, he was even more afraid, and he went back inside the palace. "Where do you come from?" he asked Jesus, but Jesus gave him no answer. "Do you refuse to speak to me?" Pilate said. "Don't you realize I have power either to free you or to crucify you?"
>
> Jesus answered, "*You would have no power over me if it were not given to you from above.*" (John 19:8–11a)

In one sentence Pontius Pilate was disabused of the notion that his authority to rule came from Tiberius, the reigning emperor. Rather, Jesus taught, Pilate's power to rule came from "above," from the sovereign God. Even when Pilate condemned Jesus to death, he did so within the sovereign will of God.

In Romans 13 Paul lays out the implications of this teaching of Jesus for governing authorities.

> *Everyone must submit himself to the governing authorities, for there is no authority except that which God has established. The authorities that exist have been established by God.* Consequently, he who rebels against the authority is rebelling against what God has instituted, and those who do so will bring judgment on themselves. For rulers hold no terror for those who do right, but for those who do wrong. Do you want to be free from fear of the one in authority? Then do what is right and he will commend you. For he is God's servant to do you good. But

[14]William Lane, *The Gospel According to Mark* (Grand Rapids, MI: Eerdmans, 1974), 424.

> if you do wrong, be afraid, for he does not bear the sword for nothing. He is God's servant, an agent of wrath to bring punishment on the wrongdoer. *Therefore, it is necessary to submit to the authorities, not only because of possible punishment but also because of conscience.* This is also why you pay taxes, for the authorities are God's servants, who give their full time to governing. Give everyone what you owe him: If you owe taxes, pay taxes; if revenue, then revenue; if respect, then respect; if honor, then honor. (Rom. 13:1–7)

When commenting on this passage, Martin Luther pointed to the example of Jesus before Pilate to illustrate how we are to "submit . . . to the governing authorities." In 1516 he wrote, "Even though rulers are wicked and unbelieving, yet is their governmental power good (in itself) and of God. So our Lord said to Pilate, to whom He submitted Himself as a pattern for us all."[15]

The point of the foregoing discussion is that Christians are to "submit" to the authorities and laws of the state where they live (v. 1). In fact, in that verse the imperative form of "submit" is used. Paul repeats the call for submission again in verse 5, where he makes it a matter of conscience, not just to avoid punishment. Clearly the person who fears God and believes that he is sovereigny controlling the course of human events will be motivated by conscience to follow the edicts of the state unless there is a very clear conflict with the teachings of Scripture. Based on this clear instruction, I believe that citizens and foreigners should be subject to a nation's laws, and this applies to immigration laws and how one enters a country and becomes a legal resident (or citizen). Every country has such laws in order to promote an orderly society.

I grew up in Egypt in the 1950s, the child of missionary parents. They had obtained work permits and visas to live and work with Egyptian churches. We understood that we were guests and comported ourselves according to the laws, recognizing that at any time we could be asked to leave. In 1956 all British Commonwealth

[15]Martin Luther, *Commentary on the Epistle to the Romans*, trans. J. T. Mueller (Grand Rapids, MI: Zondervan, 1954), 163–164.

visa holders were forced to leave Egypt because of the political and military hostilities between the two nations. Americans were permitted to remain. In the 1970s my parents moved to Canada, but first they had to go through lengthy procedures to obtain legal immigrant status there. I did too, including a physical exam, a check of medical records, filling out countless forms, and then waiting months to hear the outcome. It would have been much easier for us to just go to Canada and take up residence, but for legal and moral reasons, going through the proper channels and adhering to the laws of Canada was the right thing to do.

In my adult years I have traveled extensively. In the mid-1980s I visited a number of former Communist countries in Eastern Europe. Despite my strong antipathy for totalitarianism and Communism, I nevertheless felt obliged to abide by the laws of the land, even those that seemed unjust to me. On one occasion I took a wrong turn while driving to West Berlin and ended up in Communist East Berlin. As it was the wee hours of the morning, we decided to stop in a large parking lot, sleep a couple of hours in the car, and then find our way out at first light. A short time later, however, police officers spotted our car because of the foreign plates and asked to see our documents. When we could not produce the proper entry visa, we were told to leave immediately. We complied.

Some countries require visitors to obtain an entry visa before arrival, while others will grant it upon arrival. In these cases, a fee is paid. Typically a country will limit how long one can stay or will place other restrictions on a visitor. For example, when I go to Egypt I have to pay a fifteen-dollar fee and am granted a maximum forty-five-day stay. When I need to extend my visit, I have to go to a government office in Cairo and pay a fee for an extension, and the new date is entered into the passport. When I depart Egypt, a military officer checks my passport to see that I have paid my fees and am leaving within the allotted period of time. If not, a heavy fine is levied. My entry visa also specifies that I cannot be employed while in Egypt.

I also frequently visit the United Kingdom. While an entry fee and visa are not required for American passport holders, one's passport is stamped with the statement that the visitor has a six-month maximum period for a visit, and it includes the following restriction: "Employment and recourse to public funding prohibited." As a visitor I must abide by these rules and can't expect the host country to allow me to be gainfully employed or to receive social benefits. Each country has the right to control who enters its borders and who is denied.

My Christian citizenship does not excuse me from the responsibilities to the laws when I visit other lands, nor does it permit me to select laws I prefer in my homeland by which to live in a different land. Rather, as Paul declared and commentators like Luther affirmed, I am obliged to submit to the laws even if I don't like them or think they are unfair or inconvenient. The advantage of living in a democracy is that one can support and vote for candidates who would bring about change that is more in keeping with one's worldview. Furthermore, one is free to lobby Congress or join political action committees to change laws, whether it has to do with immigration or any other issue.

Concerning the instruction in Romans 13 regarding the duties of the Christian to the law of his or her homeland, it is astonishing that some supporters of immigration reform or immigrants' rights treat Romans 13 rather cavalierly. One recent example of dismissive treatment of Romans 13 is found in a book by M. Daniel Carroll R.[16] He argues that the starting point on the status of illegal immigrants in America should not be a legal one that is resolved by appealing to Romans 13, which requires submitting to the laws. Rather, Carroll believes that "prior considerations" must be made before addressing the legal questions.[17] For Carroll, the starting point is that the immigrant should be viewed as being made in the image of God regardless of whether he or she has the proper legal documentation. Certainly any nation should treat visitors, legal or

[16]M. Daniel Carroll R., *Christians at the Border: Immigration, the Church and the Bible* (Grand Rapids, MI: Baker, 2008).
[17]Ibid., 131.

otherwise, with dignity and respect. As a Christian I expect that of my country. However, that does not mean that because people are made in the image of God, a subject we addressed earlier in Chapter 4, a government official or authority should look the other way when a crime is committed. There is no basis in Scripture for such a stance. On the contrary, because people are made in the image of God, there are expectations of humans. Among other things, the image of God provides each individual with the authority to have dominion over the earth (cf. Gen. 1:27–28) and therefore implies that people have the obligation of stewardship for creation.[18]

Furthermore the conscience, to which Paul appeals in Romans 13:5, is common to everyone because they are made in the image of God. That is why God in the book of Amos could judge foreign nations for invading their neighbors and causing harm.[19] Naturally, people who believe in the Bible as a source of authority should be held to an even higher standard.

A pastor friend from a Middle Eastern country told me of an interview he had given to a Muslim journalist who was writing about the implications of Sharia or Islamic law and how this would affect the Christian community should it be introduced to his country. The pastor shocked the interviewer by saying, "I have no problem. If a Christian steals something, his hand should be cut off! Christians should not steal." The pastor was not endorsing Sharia because that could allow for Christians to be severely mistreated. Rather his point was that he expected Christians to adhere to even draconian Sharia law because of the high moral standard God expects of believers. Christians, he maintained, ought to be law-abiding, moral people.

For Carroll's position to have merit, current American laws must be inherently unjust. His interest is primarily with the treatment of Hispanic "undocumented" immigrants, and he suggests

---

[18]See discussion and documentation for this in Chapter 4.

[19]In Amos 1–2 the prophet announces God's coming judgment on Israel's neighbors for various offenses and atrocities. These people knew nothing of the Sinaitic laws of Israel. Nevertheless, God expected them to uphold a minimal standard of humanitarian behavior. I assume the reason for this is because through general revelation and/or because humans are made in the image of God he holds people accountable to minimal moral expectations.

that the issue might fall under the category of laws that should be ignored and then quotes Acts 4:19 (see below) as if God's laws conflict with American immigration laws.[20] In the data amassed in theses chapters, I see nothing in Scripture that would abrogate current immigration laws.

## GOD'S LAW VS. SECULAR LAW

Let us return to the matter of secular versus scriptural law. What if the laws are truly immoral or unethical? That is, what if the existing laws truly conflict with the plain teaching of Scripture? Occasionally there will be a conflict between the laws of the secular state and a biblical law or principle that is a clear violation of conscience. A number of stories in the Bible illustrate such conflicts.

The Hebrew midwives during the oppression in Egypt, for example, were confronted with a moral dilemma: obey Pharaoh's edict to kill newborn Israelite baby boys or comply with higher law and respect life (cf. Exod. 1:15–16). They opted, as the text reports, to "fear God" and defied Pharaoh and refused to commit infanticide. As a consequence, God rewarded them (Exod. 1:17–21). In the end Pharaoh may have recognized his own excesses because he did not punish their insubordination. Clearly they chose to preserve human life rather than participate in an evil program.

Earlier the narrative of the wise men who visited baby Jesus was mentioned (Matt. 2). They did not return to Herod to report where they found the Christ as ordered by the monarch because they learned in a dream what that ruler's motives were. They refused to aid the despot in his plot to kill young Jesus. So the text records that they returned to their homeland by a different route (Matt. 2:12), thus disobeying the king but honoring God. From the text we plainly see that their defiance was authorized by a God-given dream.

We read in the book of Acts that a quandary arose for the apostles when they were instructed by the Jewish authorities not to preach in the name of Jesus. Peter and John responded by say-

[20]Carroll, *Christians at the Border*, 132.

ing, "Judge for yourselves whether it is right in God's sight to obey you rather than God. For we cannot help speaking about what we have seen and heard" (Acts 4:19–20). So there are clearly situations when a Christian may on moral grounds object to the laws and orders from governmental authorities and in good conscience resist such laws.

A modern example might be that of medical professionals who in their training or practice are called upon to perform abortions but refuse to take a life on moral grounds. Some years ago there was a case of a nurse who found a live aborted fetus in a hospital. The law at the time demanded that no assistance be given to help the baby live. She defied the law and helped the neonate even though that created a legal dilemma for herself.

The examples in Scripture, as well as the modern cases cited here, of rejecting secular law in favor of clear biblical teaching or because of conscience usually entail the preservation of life. In the case of the apostles in Acts 4, the issue was freedom for Christians to proclaim the gospel (cf. Matt. 28:19–20; Acts 1:8). Surely breaking immigration laws to improve one's economic standard does not rise to the same moral level as a medical professional refusing to perform an abortion. Thus I believe that Carroll's attempt to equate American immigration laws as an example of a conflict between secular and sacred law is a matter of special pleading.

## "I WAS A STRANGER AND YOU INVITED ME IN"

A final area of the New Testament that should be considered includes the teachings of Jesus concerning the gracious treatment of needy people. Jesus' teaching in Matthew 25:31–46 and especially verses 35–36 is frequently offered as a case for Christian ethics. Here he said, "For I was hungry and you gave me something to eat, I was thirsty and you gave me something to drink, I was a stranger and you invited me in, I needed clothes and you clothed me, I was sick and you looked after me, I was in prison and you came to visit me." This Scripture has no comparable passage in the other Gospel accounts. Jesus in Matthew 25:31–46 portrays the final judgment when the king, understood to mean Jesus himself when he returns,[21] receives those who will inherit "the kingdom." Following the invitation by the king, he explains that it was because of the kindnesses extended to him by the righteous (enumerated in vv. 35–36) that they were included. The righteous people are incredulous: "Lord, when did we see you hungry and feed you . . ." (vv. 37–39). The king responds by saying, "I tell you the truth, whatever you did for *one of the least of these brothers of mine*, you did for me" (v. 40).

This passage has elicited considerable discussion among New Testament commentators. The crux of the problem is identifying the recipients of the acts of kindness who are called "the least of these brothers of mine." Who are the brothers of the king or of Jesus whose treatment is at issue? Early sages like St. Jerome (fourth century A.D.) and a host of others to the present time have wrestled with this question, resulting in no less that eight different interpretations![22] Of these, only four (or combinations of the four) continue to be seriously considered by exegetes:

1. Anyone who is needy, i.e., all humanity, advocated by theologians like Jerome, Augustine, Chrysostom, and Zwingli and more recent scholars like Gundry, Davies, and Allison.[23]
2. All Christians, a position favored by earlier thinkers like Prosper of Aquitaine and Caesarius of Arles and recently by V. P. Furnish.[24]
3. The apostles or disciples of Christ and other missionaries, a view held by J. R. Michaels, J. Mánek,[25] and R. Mounce.[26]
4. The apostles or the disciples whom Christ sent out, a position supported largely by more recent expositors, e.g.,

[21]Ulrich Luz, *Matthew 21–28* (Minneapolis: Fortress, 2005), 277.
[22]W. D. Davies and D. C. Allison, *The Gospel According to Saint Matthew*, Chapters XIX-XXVIII (Edinburgh: T&T Clark, 1997), 422) offers a list of six views and the various interpreters of those positions, and D. A. Carson includes some of those and adds others held by evangelical Christians (Carson, *Matthew*, *Expositor's Bible Commentary*, 8 [Grand Rapids, MI: Zondervan, 1984], 518–520).
[23]See the list in ibid., 422.
[24]See Davies and Allison, *The Gospel According to Saint Matthew*, 422.
[25]Reviewed in Carson, *Matthew*, 519.
[26]Robert H. Mounce, *Matthew* (San Francisco: Harper & Row, 1976).

> L. Morris[27] and U. Luz[28] and including Roman Catholic scholars such as D. Senior.[29] D. A. Carson holds this view but secondarily extends the application to other Christians.[30]

That Jesus is referring to all humanity is not only an interpretation that Christians have taken since the early Christian era, but currently some churches and organizations embrace this understanding. A Christian humanitarian relief organization actually calls itself Matthew 25 Ministries. Their mission, according to their website (m25m.org), "is to fulfill Matthew 25:34–40 by providing nutritional food to the hungry, clean water to the thirsty, clothing to the naked, shelter to the homeless, medical care to the ill, and humanitarian supplies to prisoners." Their work is directed primarily at "the poorest of the poor locally, regionally, nationally and internationally regardless of race, creed or political persuasion."

These are laudable goals, but this all-inclusive interpretation of Matthew 25:40, 45 is problematic because the New Testament nowhere refers to all humanity as the "brothers of Jesus." As Carson observes, "there is no parallel for this."[31] Those who prefer the fourth or the third position, which is an extension of the fourth, dismiss the second position that all Christians are intended because in Matthew the term *brothers* (*adelphoi*) refers specifically to his disciples (cf. Matt. 12:48–49; 28:10).[32] In other words, Matthew uses "brothers" in a specialized and restrictive manner.

Even Carroll recognizes this interpretation when he says that the stranger in Matthew 25:35, 38 "is technically a disciple who goes to another land for ministry and thus is a foreigner there."[33] He goes on to affirm, "I do not make a one-to-one correspondence between the disciples of Matthew 25 and all Hispanic

---

[27]Leon Morris, *The Gospel According to Matthew* (Grand Rapids, MI: Eerdmans, 1992), 639.
[28]Luz, *Matthew 21–28*, 279–280.
[29]Donald Senior, *The Gospel of Matthew* (Nashville: Abingdon Press, 1997), 163.
[30]Carson, *Matthew*, 520.
[31]Ibid., 519.
[32]Luz, *Matthew 21–28*, 279–280.
[33]Carroll, *Christians on the Border*, 124.

immigrants."[34] But then in an about-face Carroll raises questions that imply that this passage should apply to the present situation, declaring that because many of the immigrants are needy, "does the Christian church of the host culture not have some responsibility to help 'the least of these brothers' in the name of Jesus?" and "Will the Son of Man and the Father in any way demand an accounting of this country's actions toward Christian Hispanics?"[35]

Here it seems that Carroll acknowledges whom specifically Jesus means in Matthew 25, and yet he wants to make an exception to include "Christian Hispanics." The interpretive double standard is apparent. I agree with Carroll that Christians and churches should seek to help the needy in practical ways. The Matthew 25 reference to feeding the hungry and taking in the foreigner, however, cannot be used to make that case without distorting what Jesus had in mind, and certainly it should not be used in determining federal policy.

Indeed Christ did feed the hungry (twice) and heal the sick (frequently), and that model for compassion is an important Christian virtue. But Carroll has clouded the issue by not distinguishing legal from illegal immigrants vis-à-vis the responsibility of government. The critical question we are addressing here is, what biblical guidelines concerning aliens (legal and illegal) should influence national immigration law? As I have shown in earlier chapters, biblical law does differentiate the legal alien (*ger*) from the foreigner (*nekhar*) who does not have resident status (see Chapters 2–4). While the former could receive social benefits under the Torah, the latter was excluded.

Does this biblical distinction mean that the Christian should only help legal aliens and spurn illegal immigrants? Obviously the starting point for Christians should be the recognition that all humans are made in the image of God, and we should seek to love our neighbor as ourselves (Lev. 19:18; Matt. 5:43; 19:19; 22:39) and to treat the needy with dignity and compassion. But this ethic

---

[34]Ibid.
[35]Ibid.

does *not* mean that Christians turn a blind eye to those who violate the law, whether the issue is immigration, robbery, identity theft, or other transgressions of the law.

Some time ago I was approached on a Sunday morning by a couple of people at the entrance of the church where I have served as an elder for many years. They said they needed food, but the food pantry was closed. I opened my wallet and found a five dollar bill, which I gave them, and they left. I did not ask about their residency status. Their need appeared to be genuine to me. If, however, they had said, "We need money or work, but we can't find employment because we lack a temporary worker (H-1b) visa or a green card," I would have tried to help with their immediate need (food) while at the same time addressing their residence status. I would fall back on the advice I gave George over thirty years ago (see Preface): do what it takes to legalize your residency, even if that means leaving the country and applying for a H-1b visa or green card. If they were Christians, I would remind them that Romans13:1 is clear that "everyone must submit himself to the governing authorities." In my view, there is no need to drive a wedge between the New Testament's teaching about being compassionate to people and the state's responsibility to enforce its laws and provide for its citizens.

An example comes to mind where care for individuals and adhering to the law did not conflict. A family from a West African country joined our church some years ago when the father and husband was finishing up a graduate degree. As his program ended, he had planned to return to Africa, but civil strife in his country posed a serious problem. Friends at home urged him not to return at that time. However, his student visa was going to expire. As he was uncertain what to do, he spoke with the elders of the church, and we decided to have him see a lawyer who specialized in immigration law to learn about changing the residency status for him and his family. We even covered a large portion of the legal fees. The outcome was that he received the necessary changes and lives legally in Illinois but hopes to return to his country in the near future. This story illustrates that churches can work to assist immigrants, legal or illegal, to have legal standing.

Thus while the New Testament does not directly speak to the legal status of immigrants and aliens and how they should be treated by a host nation, it does set forth two important principles. The first is that governments are ordained by God, and laws and ordinances made by humans, unless they clearly violate divine principles or teaching, should be followed. The second is that Christians themselves are considered aliens in this world, and their attitude toward others should be, as Paul instructs, "as we have opportunity, let us do good to all people, especially to those who belong to the family of believers" (Gal. 6:10).

Chapter 9

# WHAT DOES THIS MEAN TODAY?

We have come to the end of our survey of the most pertinent biblical passages that in some way touch on immigration and aliens. It seems fitting to conclude this book by drawing together some of the most salient observations we have already made and discussing their implications for nations and governments, immigrants, employers, and churches and religious institutions. The Bible has something to say to each.

## NATIONS AND GOVERNMENTS

At the outset of this study it was observed that nation states large and small in the biblical world were clearly delineated by borders that were often defended by large forts and military outposts (Chapter 2). Israel, too, had distinct borders that God prescribed (Gen. 15:18) and are described in incredible detail in Joshua (13–19) where the subunits or tribal territories of Israel are recorded. From ancient times to the present, the borders of countries were respected, and minor skirmishes and even wars followed when people or armies of one nation violated the territory of their neighbor.

Countries since biblical times have had the right to clearly established secure borders that they controlled and were recognized by surrounding governments, traveling tribes, and individuals. Furthermore, nations, including Israel of the Bible, had the right to determine who entered their land and under what circumstances, and they could confer resident or alien status to foreigners should it be mutually beneficial. The same is true today, I maintain.

Nations that receive aliens must not at some future time turn against them and mistreat them as the Egyptians did the Israelites (Chapter 3). There has been a tendency to do this in recent centuries during times of economic hardship for the host nation. Americans may recall the illegal and inhumane treatment of Japanese Americans during World War II. Immigrant groups are often targeted and blamed for a crisis! Biblical law is unambiguous that when people were accepted in Israel, the alien had to be treated fairly in legal and social spheres. Ancient Israel had experienced being received as aliens or *gerim* in the book of Genesis, only to be turned into slaves of the state in the book of Exodus. The laws in the Torah were intended to prevent Israel from doing the same to aliens in their midst.

### *Legal Areas*

The laws of the Torah are not always directly applicable to a modern secular society. However, the fact that God introduced laws and statutes demonstrates that the rule of law for governments to enforce is essential (Chapters 3–4) and should be respected by citizens, aliens, and foreign visitors.

Equal justice under the Law applied to the alien and citizen alike in Israel. The laws of the Bible were to be equally applied to citizen and alien (Num. 15:15–16). We should expect equal application of local, state, provincial, and federal laws. In the court system there should be no partiality shown, and judges must be fair (cf. Deut. 1:15–17; 27:19).

Our review of the practice of sanctuary revealed that the alien, like the Israelite, could seek legal protection from the law of retaliation only in cases of involuntary manslaughter (see Chapter 4). Offenders of other crimes, including premeditated murder, did not qualify to take refuge at the sanctuary or one of the legally mandated locations around the country of Israel. The only modern application of the biblical practice of sanctuary is to be sure that an offender gets a fair hearing before an impartial court, and a change of venue should be extended to a defendant if a fair trial cannot be assured. Indeed in the American legal system a defendant can request a change of venue, a request that is often heeded by the court.

Cities and municipalities who offer sanctuary for illegal aliens do so without the support of biblical law. Because biblical sanctuary was only intended to allow the innocent party to get a fair hearing and trial, and not for the purpose of sheltering lawbreakers from the authorities and agents of the state, cities that provide a safe haven for illegal immigrants, while intending to be a gesture of justice, are in fact violating federal law and are misappropriating biblical law.

### *Social Areas*

The law was specific that "the alien living with you must be treated as one of your native-born" (Lev.19:34) and therefore was eligible for social benefits (Lev. 19:9–10; Deut. 26:12–13). Today aliens (i.e., legal immigrants) who are needy should be extended governmental social services such as welfare, unemployment, food stamps, job training, and other benefits offered to disadvantaged citizens. Aliens and their children should qualify for public education and tuition breaks like in-state residents. As in biblical law, the legal alien should receive the same social benefits as a citizen. However, as the gleaning laws remind us, the poor and the aliens actually had to go out and work in the fields to get the grains and fruits (Lev. 19:9–10; 23:22; Deut. 24:19–21). In the story of Ruth we gain an appreciation for the effort that gleaning required, laboring from morning to evening (Ruth 2:1–19). This suggests that there is nothing inappropriate in expecting those who benefit from the generosity of others and the state to expend some effort in meeting their own needs.

## IMMIGRANTS

In our investigation of the book of Genesis we learned that during the early second millennium B.C. when Abraham, Isaac, and Jacob and their families traveled between Mesopotamia and Egypt and throughout ancient Canaan, they encountered countries and city-states that had recognized and often defended borders (Chapter 2). As a consequence the Israelites when traveling between regions had to respect the territorial integrity of these nations, and they even had to obtain permission simply to transit through a land (cf. Num. 20:16–21). The Genesis patriarchs even drafted legal agreements or treaties with their hosts that allowed them to stay within their territories and have access to water sources for their flocks (Gen. 21:22–34; 26:1–33). When Abraham lied to Egyptian authorities about his marital status and the identity of Sarah, his wife, he was expelled from Egypt.

Additionally, we examined in detail the Hebrew terms for alien (*ger*) and foreigner (*nekhar* and *zar*). The *ger*, it is evident, was an immigrant who took up residence in a foreign land with the permission of a host. Nowhere in the Old Testament is there any sense that a nation had to accept immigrants, nor was being received as an alien a right. That permission was required for a foreigner to reside in another land is illustrated in the case of Jacob's family who via Joseph (an official in Pharaoh's court) received permission to sojourn in Egypt (Gen. 45:16–20), which was followed by Joseph's brothers asking Pharaoh for authorization to bring their families and flocks to the eastern delta (Gen. 47:1–6).

The *ger* in the Bible, I maintain, corresponds to a legal alien today. In Chapter 4 it was shown that aliens had rights within Israelite society that were denied to the foreigner. Carrying this principle over to the present day, I conclude that the legal alien ought to have most of the rights of citizenship (voting and serving on juries are current exceptions). Meanwhile, illegal immigrants should not expect these same privileges from the state whose laws they disregard by virtue of their undocumented status.

The Bible clearly distinguishes between the status of a legal alien (*ger*) and a foreigner (*nekhar* and *zar*), and one consequence of this is that there really is a difference between the legal standing of a present-day documented alien and an illegal immigrant.

Therefore it is legally and morally acceptable for a government to deal with those in the country illegally according to the nation's legal provisions. The Christian insists, however, that they be dealt with in a humane manner. Expatriation (as Abraham experienced) in itself is not inhumane, but it must not be done in a heartless manner.

In the previous chapter we discussed the dearth of New Testament passages dealing with immigrants. Paul's instruction about submitting to the laws of a nation, articulated in Romans 13, is germane to the citizen, legal alien, and illegal alien alike. The apostle declares, "Everyone must submit himself to the governing authorities, for there is no authority except that which God has established. The authorities that exist have been established by God" (Rom. 13:1). Most of the illegal immigrants in the USA come from Central and South America where the vast majority are Roman Catholics or Protestant Christians as Daniel Carroll reminds us.[1] As such, they need to be sensitive to their obligation to this teaching of Scripture and work through what may be deemed to be imperfect government procedures to obtain legal status in the land to which they hope to immigrate.

## EMPLOYERS

One of the main attractions for those who emigrate is to improve their economic standing by seeking better employment. Unfortunately, there have been too many cases in America of unethical employers taking advantage of aliens in general and illegal immigrants in particular. However, the Bible is manifestly clear that like other workers, aliens should be paid on time and according to the standard rates (Deut. 24:14–15). Employers who discriminate against workers because they are perceived to be powerless and lack legal protection and consequently pay them below the standard wage need to be appropriately sanctioned and fully prosecuted. Romans13 applies to bosses too!

[1]M. Daniel Carroll R. makes this observation in *Christians at the Border: Immigration, the Church and the Bible* (Grand Rapids, MI: Baker, 2008), Chapter 1 and elsewhere.

Exploitation of illegal immigrants by employers for less compensation is bad enough, but this practice also can result in depriving citizens and legal aliens of what would be better paying jobs. Furthermore, when employees are paid "off the books" as is the case with many illegal immigrants, the state is deprived of revenue. Hence employers are obliged morally and legally to follow the rule of law and the ethical principles of the Bible by treating alien and citizen alike in hiring and compensation.

## CHURCHES AND RELIGIOUS INSTITUTIONS

People who take the teachings of Scripture seriously and want to treat people graciously will no doubt struggle to find an ethical and legal balance between helping those who are needy on the one hand and yet are residing in the nation illegally on the other. Then too one must accept the fact that the Old Testament law draws a distinction between the legal alien and the foreigner. Consequently the Christian will continue to wrestle with being compassionate and yet recognizing that illegal immigrants, like themselves, need to submit to the laws of the land. Despite this quandary, there are plenty of foreigners, refugees, and immigrants who legally reside in America, Canada, or Britain whom churches and religious institutions can assist.

One of the areas where a direct correlation does not work in a modern secular state is in religious matters introduced in the Torah. Ancient Israel was a religiously based community from which flowed its social and legal traditions. Religious inclusion in ancient Israel began when the alien males were circumcised as a sign of their inclusion in the covenant community and were in submission to the legal code of the Torah (Exod. 12:48). The inclusion of the alien in the religious life of ancient Israel shows that critical to the assimilation of foreigners into a new society was their incorporation into a religious community. Secular governments cannot and should not do this.

There is no doubt that religious organizations are the key to welcoming new citizens, aliens, and refugees. Once the aliens were initiated religiously in biblical Israel, they were free to participate in the worship of the community and in the various religious festivals and holy days. What can churches and other religious communities learn from the principles in the Hebrew Scriptures about incorporating the alien into their congregations? Even without formal membership, churches can welcome foreign guests, extend friendship, and help in practical ways.

With this in mind the church where I was a member is intentionally multi-ethnic. The vision statement reads: "Bridgeway Community Church desires to glorify God by proclaiming the Gospel and making disciples within a loving, multi-cultural community that serves the people of Southeast Carol Stream and surrounding areas, in all their diversity, in order for all people to come to a saving and growing knowledge of Jesus Christ."[2] This church, along with others in the area, offers classes in English as a second language free of charge to newcomers to America who need to learn English. These individuals are assisted with cultural assimilation as well as religious incorporation should they choose to attend services. Services at Bridgeway Community Church regularly include songs in other languages—recently Spanish, Russian, and Chinese choruses have been sung. Greetings and Bible verses in different languages are printed in the weekly bulletin. These are small measures, but they have a welcoming effect.

In the previous chapter I recounted the case of one immigrant family that the church assisted financially to consult an immigration lawyer who was able to help them change their immigrant status so they could lawfully stay in the country. There are many ways religious and charitable organizations can help aliens with their transition to life in their new home and thus follow the spirit of the teachings of the Bible. As suggested here in this concluding chapter, organizations can aid illegal immigrants in lawful ways. But the practice of sanctuary for illegal immigrants, just as in the case of municipalities, should not be used by Jewish and Christian organizations thinking they are following the biblical tradition of

[2]See the church website, www.bwcc.org.

the cities of refuge (see Chapter 4). As we have shown, *sanctuary* had a very specific legal function, and it was not to protect people from the law but to ensure that they received a fair trial in cases of accidental death. It might be appropriate for a church, however, to serve as a mediator between lawbreakers and authorities to help the defendants understand their rights and due process.

## CONCLUSION

This book obviously is not meant to be the final word from the Bible on the subject of immigration and the plight of illegal aliens. Rather it is my hope that the thoughts offered here are based on relevant biblical passages and that some of their implications for the current debate on immigration will be helpful to the readers of this book. If people and institutions believe that current immigration laws in America or any other country need to be reformed to better accommodate the needs of the nation and immigrants alike, then the democratic process needs to be followed. While the deliberations take place, many of the teachings of the Bible and its principles discussed here could prove constructive to the national discourse.

# ILLUSTRATION CREDITS

Figure 1: From *The ESV Study Bible*. Copyright © 2008 by Crossway Bibles, a publishing ministry of Good News Publishers. Used by permission. All rights reserved.

Figure 2: From *The ESV Study Bible*. Copyright © 2008 by Crossway Bibles, a publishing ministry of Good News Publishers. Used by permission. All rights reserved.

Figure 3: From *The ESV Study Bible*. Copyright © 2008 by Crossway Bibles, a publishing ministry of Good News Publishers. Used by permission. All rights reserved.

Figure 4: P. Newberry, *Beni Hasan* I (London, 1893), pl. 31.

Figure 5: P. Newberry, *Beni Hasan* I (London, 1893), pl. 38.

Figure 6: Courtesy of the Brooklyn Museum.

Figure 7a: Photograph by James K. Hoffmeier.

Figure 7b: Photograph by Heather Alexander.

Figure 8: W. S. Smith, *Art and Architecture of Ancient Egypt* (Baltimore: Penguin, 1958), 101.

Figure 9: Norman de Garis Davies, *The Tomb of Rekhmire at Thebes* (New York: Metropolitan Museum, 1943), pl. 47.

Figure 10: Copyright Mission archéologique franco-égyptienne de Tell el-Herr; d'après D. Valbelle (dir.), Tell el-Herr. Les niveaux hellénistiques et du Haut-Empire, Paris, 2007, p. 15, fig. 7.

Figure 11a: Photograph by James K. Hoffmeier.

Figure 11b: Photograph by James K. Hoffmeier.

# SCRIPTURE INDEX

## *Leviticus*



## *Numbers*

# GENERAL INDEX